MW01231265

Almost Already

INSECURITIES, FAILURES, AND OTHER
FUN THINGS NOBODY LIKES TO TALK ABOUT

ALMOST ALREADY

INSECURITIES, FAILURES, AND OTHER
FUN THINGS NOBODY LIKES TO TALK ABOUT

JONATHAN TONY

© 2018 by Jonathan Tony

Printed and distributed in the United States of America

All rights reserved. No part of this publication may be reproduced, stored in a retrieval system, or transmitted in any form or by any means—for example, electronic, photocopy, recording—without the prior written permission of the author. The only exception is brief quotations in reviews.

ISBN-13: 978-0692136478 (Jonathan Tony) ISBN-10: 0692136479

Unless otherwise stated, Scripture quotations are from the Holy Bible, New International Version®, NIV® Copyright © 1973, 1978, 1984, 2011 by Biblica, Inc.® Used by permission. All rights reserved worldwide.

Scripture taken from *Holy Bible*, New Living Translation, copyright © 1996, 2004, 2015 by Tyndale House Foundation. Used by permission of Tyndale House Publishers, Inc., Carol Stream, Illinois 60188. All rights reserved.

Cover design by Ben Lopez.

Editing by Brittany Tony, LeAna Kimball, and Steffan Clousing.

To Ella

May you be full of confidence in who you are and what you're worth, and may you grow to know how much your Creator loves you. Luckily, no one in your family has any insecurities or issues so you should be good to go.

Uncle J

Contents

Chris Traegar: "The key to April's heart is within you, Andy. You need to tap into the aspects of your personality that she once found attractive to make yourself the best version of yourself. What's great about you?"

Andy Dwyer: "I'm nice."

Chris Traegar: "Good! Nice. What else?"

Andy Dwyer: "I'm in a band."

Chris Traegar: "Band! What else?"

Andy Dwyer: "That's it."[1]

Parks and Recreation

Chapter 1

We Started from the Bottom and We're Still There

This is the First Chapter in the Book

"That was the low point. Flipping out over four hotdog buns. I couldn't figure out why I'd gotten so nuts."[1]

George Banks, *Father of the Bride*

I'm going to fight Chip and Joanna Gaines.

Yeah, I said it. I'm coming for you two. Don't sit there and laugh at me. Wipe that smirk off your perfect, beautiful, made-for-TV faces. I'm serious. I'll do it.

Sigh.

Alright, I'm not really going to fight you, Chip and Joanna Gaines. You don't deserve my wrath. And by "wrath" I mean me closing my eyes and swinging my fists aimlessly while singing "Eye of the Tiger."

It's just . . . why do you have to be so awesome? Why do you have to make home improvement look so easy and fun? You're selling us lies. Everyone knows house projects began when Adam and Eve got kicked out of the Garden of Eden as a punishment from God. It's why Jesus was a carpenter; he had to prove he was the most patient man of all time. No better way to prove that than by assembling a bookshelf.

So, Chip and Joanna—can I call you *Choanna*?

Choanna, I apologize, but I haven't had as much fun doing home projects with my wife. You guys crack jokes and give each other playful smiles, whereas my wife, Brittany, usually avoids my work area altogether. If we really want to put our marriage to the test, she helps me with a project, and we spend the next few hours primarily speaking through passive aggressive sentences.

"Yes. That would be a good idea, wouldn't it? That is why I already tried it."

"It's fine. I'll get it. Don't worry about it."

"No, you are definitely not becoming your mother."

Last year we bought a house together, and so it fills me with great pride to be able to tell everyone we're still married. Don't get me wrong, we love each other very much and genuinely like each other, but there are moments of great trial brought on by home projects. I often face my highest levels of stress when attempting to do things I've never done and expecting everything to go flawlessly.

I'm new to the world of home repairs and wood projects. I became interested in woodworking a few years ago when Brittany and I first got married. That is, if you can even call what I do now woodworking. It's more like building rudimentary shelves with only right angles. I was putting together a ton of furniture for our new apartment, like bookshelves and tables we'd gotten from Wayfair and Ikea, and it became therapeutic for me to work a little with my hands after a day of sitting in front of a computer at the office. It was like adult Legos. Once I completed assembling all of our store-bought furniture, I wanted to keep building. So, I thought woodworking would be satisfying. I like making practical items I can use and look at later. Like a table, or chairs, or shelving reinforcements for the times when Brittany puts too many hangers on our wire shelves in the closet and they rip off the wall in the middle of the night and we think someone is breaking into our house. Did you know yelling, "I know you're there, dude!" isn't as threatening as it sounds, especially when it's yelled into an empty closet?

I've managed to fumble my way through enough projects to fool people into thinking I know what I'm doing. Truthfully, I watch YouTube videos and then guess my way through the tasks. I haven't electrocuted myself yet, but if you come to our house and wonder why we have some pictures and paintings on the wall in random, off-centerplaces, it's most likely because we are covering up a hole I made while trying to put in a drywall anchor. DIY means "Do It Yourself," but I like to just pronounce it as "DIE" because that's a more accurate statement of how I feel whenever I'm in the middle of a DIY project.

Brittany calls me a handyman, and I appreciate it, but I'm sad her standards of what qualifies as "handy" are so low. Recently, she wanted to replace the chandelier in our home and spent a long time picking out just the right one— something modern and rustic that also says, "We're farmers in the 19th century." I said, "Sure. I think I can do that." Then, like an idiot who had watched too much of Choanna, I asked her, "Can you help me install it?" Brittany hesitantly said she would, seeming to know how this DIE project would end up going.

Up to that point, my knowledge of installing chandeliers began and ended at changing a light bulb. I didn't grow up working on many projects with my dad. The only projects I remember working on with him were holding up our lawn mower so he could sharpen the blades and the one time we put together a model car I'd gotten for Christmas when I was a kid. I remember starting to put the pieces of the car together and then falling asleep on the couch. I woke up to a shiny red Corvette my dad had finished without me. What a wonderful, bonding experience that was. Thanks, Dad. Gee, I wonder why I'm writing a book about self-esteem?

YouTube has become my father now, as I'm sure it has to many a lost boy like me. I went online and looked up what I could find about the process of installing a chandelier. After watching a few videos, I thought, "I can do this. Seems simple enough."

It never is, is it? People like Choanna make us believe we are capable of this kind of crap and that we'll even enjoy it. It's like when someone has the idea on a vacation, "Oh we should go canoeing!" Then seven hours later, when you're exhausted and covered in sunburns and contemplating leaving your kids in the woods, you realize how much you hate nature and all of its stupid beauty. Canoeing seemed like such a good idea at first, as do all DIE projects.

The chandelier swap involved some electrical work, so that definitely upped the ante for me. I don't do much electrical work, but whenever I do, it always adds more pressure and stress to the project. It's one thing to pinch your finger, it's a whole other mess if you electrocute yourself and set the house on fire. One time I changed a power outlet and I felt like I was Tom Cruise defusing a bomb in a *Mission Impossible* movie.

After my quick download of information and instructions, I told Brittany, "This should take about 30 minutes at most." I turned off the power breakers and started removing the old chandelier.

Three hours later, we weren't speaking to each other.

What should have been a simple *unscrew-this-then-screw-that-in* project became a Murphy's Law nightmare. When installing chandeliers with essentially no idea what you're doing, you have a limited amount of time with which to work because you're standing on a ladder and trying to hang it in the middle of the ceiling. You can't put part of it together, set it down, and then step back and think about your next step. You have to plan as best you can for what is going where and what you think will happen and then execute it to the best of your ability all at once while one person holds up the chandelier. All the pressure mounts, and it becomes a test of composure and fearlessness. It's like ordering a pizza over the phone.

The old chandelier came down easily, and I didn't electrocute myself, which made me feel like I was off to a good start. *Hmm, maybe I should have my own home renovation show?* I went up on the ladder, and Brittany climbed up the other side of the ladder and lifted the chandelier up as high as she could so I could connect the wires and then start screwing in the base plate. Unfortunately, Brittany goes for tone and not bulk when she lifts weights, so all we had were 15-second bursts where she was able to hold the chandelier up high enough for me to try and install it. I repeatedly connected the wrong wires, and the screws wouldn't go into the settings in the ceiling. I'd quickly unscrew it, disconnect the wires, and set it back down on the floor while we regrouped.

This went on for about three hours. Every time we'd try, there would be some piece that was off or not complying in some way. The existing mount wasn't connecting with the mount of the new chandelier. It felt like the chandelier parts were actively working against me. Mocking me. Putting a "Kick-Me" sign on my back and stealing my lunch money. Calling me names like Doofus and Not-Good-At-Stuff Boy.

They weren't particularly clever insults, but it still hurt my feelings.

I've heard it said over and over: "Never go to bed angry." Personally, I don't agree with that advice. I think most times when tensions are high and we are tired from a long day, we should just call it quits and get some sleep. Lack of sleep isn't helping anything. Your nerves are shot, and everything seems more intense when you're tired and cranky.

That said, I ignored my own anti-advice and decided to stay up and fight through the installation. What would Tom Cruise do? I kept thinking I was two minutes away from finishing it, but it continued to get more annoying. Sinking deeper and deeper into misery, the harder I struggled, the worse it got. Like a Chinese finger trap. Or like ordering pizza over the phone and asking if you can use a coupon.

The sun was up when we started our little home project, but as the hours rolled on, I had to plug in a shop light with an extension cord so we could see what we were doing. I was standing near the top of my ladder when our dog, Walter, spontaneously and loudly barked at something he heard outside. It spooked me, and I almost fell off. I yelled at him more fiercely than I ever have before. He ran and hid from me for awhile. Then, I started speaking more aggressively to Brittany. My temper came out in a humiliating and embarrassing way. I didn't throw things at her or anything like that, but she fell under my wrath. It wasn't anger that was even directed at her; it was directed at myself, but she was caught in the crossfire.

Do you ever have those out-of-body moments where you are standing outside of yourself, watching yourself do something you wish you could stop? *Alternate You* is thinking, "Please, just stop. Don't do this. Don't go there. You can shut this down. Stop, you idiot!" But by that point, you have too much momentum to stop. You fail knowing you are failing and you can't put the brakes on. I remember thinking I could control my temper if I'd just settle down and stop for the night, but instead I said, "Shut up, *Alternate Me*! I have to finish this! WHAT WOULD TOM CRUISE DO?"

Even with all that Brittany and Walter had to endure, I got it the worst. I hated myself that night. I said some things to myself and about myself I can't ever imagine saying to anyone else. Repeatedly hating myself and calling myself a loser, a failure, and much worse. I was mad at the chandelier, and then I was mad at myself for being mad. I hated myself for losing my temper, and that made me even angrier.

No one likes to struggle through something. But if you are like me and you battle your pride and insecurity at the same time, these kinds of moments will happen. You hurt people you never wanted to hurt. You say words you can't take back. You begin to destroy a trust that took a long time to build up.

In the end, we finished the chandelier installation. Brittany didn't speak to me the rest of the night, and eventually we went to bed. Usually when I complete a project, there is a momentary high where I get to look at the work of my hands, and I get to be at least a little impressed with myself. Brittany usually comes over and excitedly admires the work, too, and it makes me feel really good. The chandelier was hung, and it actually turned on like it was supposed to. But this time, I felt no joy. I took a shower and thought through the last few hours. I was depressed. I was mad at myself for being so mad at myself. I felt like a failure of a husband. I *was* a failure of a husband. I crawled into bed next to Brittany who was lying with her back to my side. I apologized for losing it and she said, "I forgive you, but you can't do that again." I tried to continue the conversation and make a few more strides toward peace, but she said she was done and going to sleep.

The next morning, there was a palpable tension in our home. We don't normally wake up singing love songs, as neither of us are morning people, but we at least acknowledge each other and normally share a hug and kiss on the cheek. People who kiss on the lips before brushing their teeth are weird. But there was no hugging or cheek kissing on that morning. I avoided her, and she avoided me. At least Walter had forgiven me and was nice to me, or maybe he just wanted his breakfast.

After a while, Brittany and I finally spoke to each other. I apologized again and told her, "I don't think that is who I am. I am not an angry person."

She said, "I think maybe you are. This isn't the first time I've seen you blow up."

"Just because I have a moment or two of weakness doesn't mean I am an angry person. I was just stressed from life at the moment, and then the chandelier made it all worse."

"Maybe. But I think you need to work through some stuff with yourself and with God. Because I'm not doing this again."

♦ ♦ ♦

Well, how's this for a first chapter? Everyone having fun? I sincerely hate sharing this story, especially as the opening of the book. This is starting out like the movie *Up*! I've been staring at the delete key for about 20 minutes now because I'm really embarrassed. I want people to think I have it together. I want to be an example of someone who is living a good life full of confidence and security. Right now, I just feel like an example of why people need therapy, or an example of why people should hire electricians.

It's humiliating to fail, but it's much worse to have your failure hurt someone else. It's one thing to trip and fall, but it's worse to trip and fall and take down the other two Jamaican sprinters who were about to qualify for the Summer Olympics and instead they now have to learn how to bobsled to compete in the Winter Olympics. (There are so many life lessons in *Cool Runnings*, aren't there?) Failure is so much harder when we bring others down with us and when our path of destruction not only ruins our lives, but also the lives of those in our wake.

Unfortunately, failure is unavoidable. If you get off the couch and attempt anything at any point in your life, you will have failures, and you will have moments of weakness. Our moments of weakness are full of meaningless actions and comments we can't remember because they seemingly make no sense. However, at the same time, they also expose what is deep inside our hearts.

I like to think I'm not an angry person, but maybe I am an angry person at my core. Just because I don't normally blow up on people in my everyday life doesn't mean that somewhere deep inside my heart there is not a rage waiting to come out. I may have built up a wall of tolerance over the years, but it doesn't mean there is not a dark creature locked behind that wall looking for a chance to escape. We all have dark beasts hiding deep in our hearts.

Jesus said, "The mouth speaks what the heart is full of."[2] So when we are under pressure, what's really inside of us will come out. Stress doesn't bring out the worst in us, it reveals the worst in us.

Eventually Brittany forgave me, and then I forgave myself. I had to spend some time repenting and thinking through why I am the way I am. Why did that chandelier get to me so much? Why did I care so much? What was I afraid of? Why did I feel so humiliated?

I was embarrassed to be having so much difficulty with it. I thought about Choanna, manly men, and friends of mine who I just assumed wouldn't have had any issues installing it, and it made me feel like a loser. I felt like I was debasing myself in front of my wife, too. I didn't want to look incompetent in her eyes. And then add all of that onto the normal exasperation one can get from tedious, frustrating homeowner tasks like these. If you end up in similar moments, you finally start to realize why you heard your dad yelling swear words at the washing machine when you were a kid.

I am a new man in many ways since that moment, and we'll discuss some of what I've been learning throughout the rest of the book. It's definitely an ongoing process; we don't change overnight. I'm learning to accept that things seldomly go according to plan. I've had other moments of stress, but I haven't reacted in the same way. I'm not saying I won't ever flip out again, but I believe I have changed and am changing.

Unfortunately, I still feel the shame and embarrassment from it. That chandelier is still hanging in our kitchen. If you come over to my house, you'll see it and now you'll know how it was installed in anger and pain. I call it my *Shamedelier*. It still stings when I look at it and think about the story of how it came to be placed there. By the way, don't ever touch it because I'm not sure how securely it was installed. Actually, just don't even look at it. Needless to say, we can't ever invite Sia over for dinner.

Maybe you don't have a chandelier of failure hanging in your home, but I'm willing to bet you have some reminders of your own failures popping up into your life now and then. A trigger for a point of weakness in your life. Some kind of portal to a past regret. Maybe it's an old picture that occasionally resurfaces on your social media. Maybe it's a child you can't look at without seeing your ex in their little face. Maybe it's your hometown that's always difficult to return to because you see shadows of your past everywhere you look. Life is full of weak moments and reminders of our failures. We all live with chandeliers hanging over our heads.

If you're a Christian like me, maybe you struggle with trying to do enough good for God. And when you fail, you feel like you have to bear your sins and hate yourself for a while so God will know you're genuinely sorry. You may think God wants you to be mad at yourself.

The truth is that God is for us.[3] He doesn't hate us when we fail, and he doesn't want us to hate ourselves. Jesus didn't die on the cross for perfect people; he died because he loved a world full of imperfect, screwed up, reckless people who let home projects get the best of them. Paul writes in Romans, "Where sin increased, grace increased all the more." We can't mess up so many times that we'll run out of his grace. It makes absolutely no sense logically, but God has forever tipped the scales in our favor. Not just tipped, but destroyed the scale entirely. That's an awesome image to think about because every time I stand on a scale I want it to be destroyed. So the next time you step on a scale and get upset that you gained three pounds over the weekend, just remember that God has destroyed the scales of justice. Also, maybe a diet with less sugar would help? Speaking of less sugar, I just started drinking LaCroix in an effort to cut back on soda. LaCroix is like a nicotine patch for soda lovers. Plus, it helps me fit in with the other moms at the pool.

God's grace cannot be earned; it can only be received. No one is ever deserving of grace. In our world, we believe in wages. You get what you work for. You want a paycheck? You have to earn it. You want to lose weight? You have to burn it. You want butter? You have to churn it. You want . . . that's all I can think of.

Grace takes that concept and demolishes it. The scale is destroyed. If God were a businessman, the Shark Tank investors would have laughed him out the door.

"God, what exactly are you profiting with this 'grace service' of yours? You are giving it out, and your clients aren't giving you anything back but filthy rags[4] and failures. I don't see a good ROI in it, and for that reason I'm out."

We have a war inside ourselves. We have that little voice, or maybe many voices, in our heads telling us we are inadequate. Maybe it's the voice of someone from your past who spoke words of disqualification over your life. Maybe your voice is someone you think may be judging your life and decisions. If you're like me, it's often your own voice. We can be the most judgmental people in our lives and our own worst enemies. My voice tends to be the loudest voice in my head, and for some reason it sounds just like Ray Romano. I can be the harshest critic in my life, like in the chandelier incident. It's one thing to battle real-life opponents and critics, but it's a totally different challenge to battle myself. I attack my own weak spots and insecurities. To battle myself means to know the deepest parts of myself.

♦ ♦ ♦

We tend to wander through life by working hard to be someone worth loving and someone worth respecting. But how do we know if we've done enough? When are we ever enough? Sometimes we think we've done enough to be someone who is valued, only to wake up the next day and feel completely worthless and alone. Each of us has insecurities and a desire to be loved and affirmed. It's normal. But just because it's normal doesn't mean it's healthy. (Alternatively, just because it's healthy doesn't mean it's normal. I'm looking at you Crossfitters.) God wants more for us. He is for us, and his grace is relentless. He's even at work right now whether we see it or not.

I want us to explore these thoughts, feelings, and burdens together. So often we feel alone in our battles, but we are never the only ones in them. There are many others fighting as well, and I hope this book helps you realize you're not alone. We will discuss insecurities, shortcomings, failures, and the lies we so easily believe, but we will also focus on God's truth.

Now let me be clear, this isn't a self-help book or science lesson. You may have gathered from the first few pages that I'm not smart enough to impart to you the psychological knowledge of why you are the way you are. There are thousands of other books out there by actual smart people who can break you down, analyze you, and give you intellectual insight on how you got so jacked up. You should probably read some of them. I don't intend for this book to be read in psychology classes, used in seminary courses, or to be on the shelf next to C.S. Lewis books. Maybe it could be placed next to a book by Richard Lewis. Or Richard Grieco. We're just going to share truth about our lives together. We're not going to clean it up or ignore the uncomfortable stuff.

I see this book as an honest conversation between friends over a cup of coffee. Or maybe we're on an awkward first Tinder date, and I suddenly just started pouring my heart out to you. Or maybe you're stuck in the seat next to me on a five-hour flight and can't get away because no one will switch seats with you. No matter how you view it, I'm glad you're here and that we can talk openly and honestly like this. Can you pick up the check, though? I forgot my wallet.

We will journey together to find who we were meant to be by discovering who God says we are—the truest version of ourselves. God's voice is not usually the loudest voice in our heads, but he should be the only voice we are listening to.

So here we go. It's going to get painfully awkward, yet surprisingly hopeful. Find out what happens when people stop being polite and start getting real.

Wait, what is that line from? I know I've heard that somewhere. *Jersey Shore*? Crap. That would have been a great ending to this chapter, but I can't end it with a line from an MTV show. I need to end this on a high note. Umm, okay, here's a picture of my dog Walter.[5]

Walter has his own Instagram account: @WaltertheFriendlyDog

Chapter 2

Overlooked

Paying My Dues and Doing My Time

GOB: "I should be in charge. I'm the older brother."
Michael: "Do you even want to be in charge?"
GOB: "No . . . But I'd like to be asked!"[1]

Arrested Development

My sister, Melissa, recently gave birth to a perfect little girl named Ella. She is the only niece or nephew I have. This uncle gig is new for me, and it's awesome. Ella and I have a lot of things in common. We both like napping, sporadically yelling nonsense, and we have the same double chin.

I don't have any kids yet, and I haven't spent a lot of time around babies, especially ones related to me, so I didn't really *get* it for a long time. I didn't understand how you could immediately love a little ball of chubbiness, but now I know there's something inexplicable about how they melt your heart. You want only the best for them, and you begin to dream of them chasing their own dreams.

So with that in mind, it must have been disheartening for my mom when she discovered my life's very first ambition.

Some of my earliest memories are waking up in the morning and spending time with my mom. She and I were usually the first awake in our home. We'd sit on our ugly red couch and watch *Mr. Rogers' Neighborhood* and *Sesame Street*. The highlight of my week, though, was when the garbage men would come pick up our trash. That's when I discovered what I wanted to do with my life. They got to ride on the back of a big truck and throw stuff into it with reckless abandon. It was the coolest! When I would hear the beeping truck turning onto our street, my mom and I would rush over to the window and watch the masters at work. We'd wave at them, and they would smile and wave back. I like to think I was the highlight of their week, too. I mean, I was an adorable ball of chubbiness.

I have nothing against garbage collectors. You can make a good living doing it, and it's honest work; it's just not one of the top choices you hear at career day in elementary schools. But neither is "inside sales representative at a health information technology company," so I'm there with you.

"What do you want to be when you grow up, Jonathan?"

"I want to cold-call hospital CFO's and aggressively be told to stop contacting them. And I want to die a little inside each time I'm rejected."

My mom never fought against my wonderment of the trash industry, but I knew she wanted something more glamorous for me. My three-year-old friend Brandon said he wanted to make paper bags, so clearly we were an ambitious crew.

Ambition is drilled into our brains from our earliest stages in life. We're taught to dream the biggest dreams possible. We can be whatever we dream up. Remember the theme song to *Reading Rainbow*? "Butterfly in the sky. I can go twice as high . . . I can be anything . . . I can go anywhere."[2]

Well, I took a look in a book, dreamed as hard as I could, and I came up with garbageman.

It's normal to pump children's heads full of ambition. You are kind of a bad parent if you don't. Kids are meant to let their imaginations run wild and to see themselves being successful in whatever they want to be. Then, when you mix in church philosophies, the dreams get even bigger and with a heavier weight of importance. You're not just dreaming of *who* you can be, you're also dreaming of *how* you can make an impact for Christ all over the world. You're not just dreaming of your own happiness and success, you're dreaming of winning souls for the Kingdom of God.

> *"You just want to be an inside sales representative and a loving husband? Dream bigger! The world needs Jesus! What you really want is to be a pastor or a missionary!"*

I'm not trying to knock the church for advocating for this approach because we do need to take the Gospel all over the world. I honestly don't know what a perfect balance of teaching on this kind of message is for kids, but I do know it's a major let down when our dreams don't become our realities. When our life's accomplishments fail to come anywhere close to our dreams, we can start giving up on dreaming. If we're a Christian, we may also feel like we have let God down.

♦♦♦

Once I outgrew my dreams of being a garbageman, I started to settle on other types of dreams. They were still big dreams, but more practical, at least. Ones I felt like I was not only capable of accomplishing, but ones I was also being called to chase. A "calling" is a term often used in the church referring to what you think God's plan is for your life.

I started performing comedy when I was in high school. I wrote funny songs and got to play them in a variety of churches, coffee houses, and fine arts competitions. Honestly, I was pretty good at it. I won awards for my performances and got more pats on the back than I could count. I wasn't an athlete or naturally very smart, but when I got the chance to make an audience laugh, I became someone I liked. Comedy gave me confidence and became my outlet, but it also became my shield and what I thought gave me value. So I got to the point where I expected to get a laugh in the majority of my conversations. If people weren't laughing, then I felt like they didn't want to be talking with me. Even right now in this book I haven't made a joke in a few minutes, and I fear you're going to stop reading.

So, Kirk Cameron walks into a bar, but then he sees a Democrat and . . . I got nothing. Please stay with me.

Comedy was my gift, but it also became a curse. I felt the pressure to be funny at all times. I think this is one of the reasons why it's common for comedians to battle with depression. A comedian is presumed to be funny, but funny is what you do, it isn't who you are. The real you goes deeper than what you give off. This applies to all of us. An athlete is praised for what they achieve on a court or field. An engineer is praised for what they can develop. These giftings and accomplishments are only a fraction of our true selves, but these fractions often become what we are most known for.

As you'd expect, my ambitious dreams morphed into doing the comedy thing full time. What if I could be a comedic evangelist? I could win so many people to Christ through the gift of humor! That became my dream. Not just because I thought it up all by myself, but because other people would tell me it was what I was going to do, which reaffirmed what I hoped to be true. "God is going to use these gifts." "God has something big for you." "I really feel like God's calling you to be a minister of his word. Pursue the calling."

I began to dream big and actively chase it down. In high school and college, I had a few promising moments where it seemed like maybe something was going to take off with my comedic evangelism, but nothing ever worked out into anything long term. I hosted some local TV and radio shows, was a youth director at my church, and even had a few big gigs doing standup comedy. None of it led to anything, or even gave me a paycheck. But I couldn't count how many times I was told, "You're paying your dues," or been quoted that verse from Zechariah, "Do not despise the days of small beginnings."[3]

Maybe my youthful ambitions will one day come to fruition, but I'm in my thirties now, and I still feel like "the days of small beginnings" are just as small as they've ever been. Perhaps even smaller now as I watch those high hopes I had fade into the distance of my past.

When you finish college and arrive at the real world, it can be a bit of a shock to many ambitious people. You realize things move a lot slower and the rewards are far fewer. For about 17 consecutive years of your life, you are rewarded year after year for your work in school by advancing to the next grade. You are given grades and awards at the end of each year, and you have extracurricular chances to win accolades, too. Our families celebrate our menial accomplishments as if we've just cured Polio. "Kevin just finished 9th grade, and we're so proud of him." "Gabby set up our TiVo for us. Watch out, Elon Musk!"

Then you graduate, and time stands still while simultaneously flying by faster than you've ever noticed it moving before. You work at the same job for three years and never get a promotion. All of a sudden you realize you're in your late twenties. Then, you look at your expanding belly and realize you can't eat pizza every day with no repercussions. You frown and then realize you're frowning twice because your neck has started to merge with your chin.

The real-world shock is depressing and it hits hard. Your big dreams tend to stall out, and you start getting mad at *Reading Rainbow* for its deception. Not to mention, if you're like me, you went to about 9,000 weddings in your first few years after college.

In my first two years after I'd graduated from college, I had a total of 11 different roommates in the apartment I lived in. I was still living in my college town of Gainesville, Florida, and I was working as a hospital valet making $5 an hour plus tips while sharing a two-bedroom apartment with three to four other guys at a time. My friend Charlie and I shared one of the two rooms, and apparently, we picked the wrong room because everyone else in the other room got married during that time except for us. Guys would move in, get engaged, and then move out. It was like Charlie and I were working at a hotel making sure everyone had a nice stay before their weddings, except we didn't leave mints on their pillows and never vacuumed.

> *"Hi, welcome to Hotel Engagement. We hope you enjoy your short stay here before you get married. We have a stove from 1972 and some of the most luxurious used couches that were left over from our previous guests who got to leave this crap hole. If you need anything, just let us know, because we'll be here until we die."*

I don't know what our problem was in Room 2, but I blame Charlie for thinking it'd be a good space saver for us to use bunk beds. Man, I wonder why no girls thought of us as marriage material? Besides saving floor space, it turns out bunk beds are a great way to remain abstinent, whether you want to or not. To this day, they are widely regarded as the safest form of birth control.

I played about every role you can at a wedding. Groomsman. Soundman. Videographer. Singer. I emceed most of them. I even performed the ceremony for two of my friends from high school, and I went stag to every single wedding. One time, I almost had a date, but she bailed on me. I think she found out about my bunk beds. I started thinking that the movie *27 Dresses* was written about my life. I'd never seen it, but I assumed she died alone in a bunk bed and still owed about $15,000 in student loans.

I felt so overlooked by God. My friends were getting married and finding jobs, seemingly without effort. At my core, I really was happy for them, but as everyone else's success was constantly happening all around me, sometimes I had to fake my excitement. Like when they zoom in on the celebrity who just lost the Academy Award and they still have to act like they are happy for the winner. I was stuck at a job I didn't like and living in a cramped apartment. I was getting older in a young town and watching the world pass me by.

"And the winner is . . . everyone else but you!"

Yes. Wonderful. Smile for the camera. This is splendid. They deserve it instead of me. Just keep clapping, dummy. Don't let them see you cry. Shove it deep, deep down inside. That's healthy. Just. Keep. Clapping.

◆ ◆ ◆

One thing we never tell kids about their dreams is that dreams also require an insane amount of luck. If you're a Christian, you can't use the word "luck," so we'll call it "giftings and connections." You must work hard, but hard work alone doesn't always make things happen.

I know this isn't a popular message, and maybe you're disagreeing with me already. I probably won't get invited to speak at any graduations for being so realistic. It's not fun to think we can't get whatever we want with a solid work ethic, a positive attitude and some grit.

I once heard NBA great Kobe Bryant speak about his success. He talked about how he worked harder than everyone else. He discussed his intense practice routines, determination, and willpower. All of that absolutely matters, and Kobe was one of the hardest working players in the league, but it probably also helped that Kobe is 6'6", built like a lion, and had parents who believed in him and supported him. I don't mean to be a cynical wet blanket here.

Note to self: Write a children's movie called The Cynical Wet Blanket about a young blanket's journey to discover he had the power to warm others the whole time. Maybe he meets Keanu Reeves along the way or something? I don't know, just run with it.

And I'm not trying to say hard work isn't important. I know there are people who overcome the odds every day by giving it all they've got. I'm just saying some people are more naturally gifted in some areas than others, and it opens doors for them that many others will never get through. We all battle our own limitations, and instead of bending the world to meet every single one of our dreams, maybe we should start accepting some of these limits. Instead of calling them limits, we could even start seeing them as guardrails that keep us from wandering off onto paths leading to destruction.

Maybe you wanted to be the next Whitney Houston, but you couldn't hit the astronomically high notes she could. So instead of becoming a world-renowned singer who, sadly, was addicted to drugs, you have lived out your life as a mother of three wonderful children who are changing the world for the better.

Maybe you wanted to be an entrepreneur whose work ethic would be written about in *Forbes Magazine*. You could have been the next superstar of business, but you were never able to get your business off the ground. You also never crashed and burned or compromised your morals in a *Wolf of Wall Street* destructive journey. Instead, you volunteer at your local church, doing what you can to meet the needs in your community.

What is your definition of success? How do you know when you've made it? When is enough really enough? When will we be satisfied?

Our culture is in love with celebrities. We elevate them up above the rest of society as examples of the ones who truly made it—the champions of the American Dream. We interview them, read their books, listen to their political advice, and wear their fashion lines available exclusively at Walmart. Jessica Simpson can't figure out where tuna fish live, but her shoes are incredible. We use celebrities' fanciful careers as a litmus test against our own. Of course, many successful people are worth learning from, but there are also many people we've deemed successful even though we don't know their whole story yet. We don't consider the end of where their path to success is taking them. At one point in time, I'm sure we thought we were getting a lot of great business advice from the heads of Enron. Then after a $40 billion lawsuit, maybe it turns out they were not the masters of business we thought they were.

Celebrities prove over and over again how screwed up their lives really are. We have heard countless times, "I thought I had it all, but I was so alone." Yet, these are the people we look to as guides to success and purpose.

I used to think it was crazy how the Israelites demanded a king to rule them in 1 Samuel. God pushed back on the idea and said they just needed to serve him and he would lead them. But they wanted a king, and apart from a few good kings here and there like David and Josiah, Israel's Old Testament history is littered with psychopathic kings. It turned out just like God told them it would.

It's crazy to think how dumb the Israelites were, yet we demand kings and queens still to this day. *Walk down the red carpet for us, King Matt Damon! Tell us who to vote for, Queen Katy Perry! Tell us who you're wearing tonight, Queen Latifah!*

We often turn celebrities into moral leaders. What is this desire we have to lift up people from the earth as gods above us? Perhaps we were created to lift someone up, but we've just picked the wrong god.

♦ ♦ ♦

As I mentioned earlier, I had dreams to be in the ministry. I thought God was grooming me, and I was paying my dues. I made sure to stay active and let God know I was ready whenever he was.

Time went on, and I was still working the same dead-end job and living in the apartment of marital blessing. I started to feel like God had forgotten about me. Like I was sitting the bench watching the more talented kids play the game.

"Coach, I'm ready whenever you need. Okay, Coach? Alright, well, I'll just be down here stretching. Does anyone need anything from the concession stand?"

I couldn't get any comedy or speaking gigs or land a job at a church. Certain friendships I thought I had turned out to be merely distant acquaintances, and my connections ended up being dead ends. Leaders I thought believed in me didn't believe in me enough to open any doors. Any time I thought, "This could be it," it never was. It was like when cartoons would draw a tunnel onto a brick wall. It looked like it was leading somewhere but always ended with me walking face first into another barrier. I couldn't get anything going for me in the world of evangelism. I felt like I had so much to share, and it was building inside of me with nowhere to go. I was a water balloon filling up under a running faucet. Remember, I had been specifically *called* to this.

I also couldn't get a job anywhere else. I was a young, inexperienced guy with a degree from the University of Florida, graduating right in the middle of a recession with no family connections and no direction. I knew a ton of people getting jobs, but I couldn't make it happen for myself.

Yes. Splendid. Just keep clapping.

During this time, that clip of Susan Boyle auditioning on *Britain's Got Talent* started circulating everywhere. I'm sure you've seen it. Out walked a frizzy-haired, spunky, middle-aged woman onto a grand stage to audition, and the audience laughed at her before she even said a word. She bantered with the judges for a moment and everyone braced themselves for another disastrous performance amongst some of the best talent in the nation. Susan started to sing "I Dreamed a Dream" from *Les Misérables* and within five seconds she'd made everyone's jaw drop with her dynamic voice. All the judges gave her a pass on to the next round and admitted they had underestimated her. Everyone was cheering for her as she wiped tears from her eyes.

I, too, saw this clip on YouTube, and I joined the audience in crying as I saw Susan live out her dream. For me, this was more than just a quaint, inspirational story. I felt like I was Susan walking out onto the stage of life, and no one was really pulling for me. No one wanted me there. I was standing up there with a silly dream and a bad haircut, baring my soul for the world.

Oh, the image of a 24-year-old man sitting alone in his apartment watching the Susan Boyle audition and crying. Let that awkwardly sit with you for a moment.

She dreamed a dream! She did it! And Simon loves her!

That stupid clip quickly became part of my "I'm feeling depressed"routine. Any time the sad feelings would creep on into my head, I'd go to watch my friend Susan dream a dream.

It sucks sitting the bench and being overlooked. Whenever we feel left out, it's a great opportunity for insecurity and pride to work together against us. For me, insecurity usually says, "You just aren't good enough, pal. No one wants you. You aren't talented enough, and you're definitely not handsome enough. Just keep clapping for everyone else. Also, that pint of ice cream ain't gonna eat itself." Then pride comes in and says, "Why should *they* get what *you* want? They haven't worked nearly as hard as you have! Their whole life has been easy. You've been faithful to God and taken high roads when you could have gone low. You're the one who deserves it! Also, that pint of ice cream ain't gonna eat itself."

Insecurity and pride are the worst friends, but they always seem to be there whether you want them or not, like weeds in your lawn or a pimple on school picture day. Or your neighbor Karen who has to knock on your door to ask you a question instead of just texting you like a normal person. These friends always show up whenever we're faced with dead ends and closed doors. They only see the negative parts of a situation, and they never speak about hope. If we let them talk too much, we'll constantly be confused and angry. Like the people who work at pizza parlors and have to take orders over the phone.

There's a popular saying amongst Christians, "When God closes a door, he opens another." Or, if you're Presbyterian, "When God closes a door, sit there and take it. It was never predestined to be opened." Or, if you're Pentecostal, "When God closes a door, break it down with your shout!" Or, if you're an atheist, you debate the existence of any door on Reddit.[4]

I believe when God closes a door, we may not see another one open immediately because it's a test of our faith or a lesson to improve our character. In the long run, it's the best for us because God knows more than we do, and we may not see the point of what was seemingly pointless for a very long time. I remember talking to my old pastor, Carl Thompson, and he told me, "There are some things it took two years for me to understand. Some things took 20 years. And there are still things I wonder about in my seventies that I don't think I'll understand until eternity."

When we say, "God, I want your plan for my life," we are submitting to his will. But it's not enough to submit just to his will, we must also submit to his timing. And as anyone who has walked with God for a few years can tell you, he operates in a different time zone than we do. It's often annoying, if I can be honest. If a door has closed, I'm standing at another door already dressed and ready to go, and God is just now getting into the shower, even though I thought we agreed on leaving at 6:30.

But since when do we know what is best for our lives? What we think are closed doors could really be divine redirection.

♦♦♦

There's a weird story right at the beginning of the book of Acts where Jesus had just left all the apostles after his resurrection, and they are in Jerusalem regrouping. Jesus had told them to wait there for the Holy Spirit to come and baptize them. There were about 120 followers of Christ in the group, including 11 of the 12 apostles who had walked with Jesus during his ministry. One of the original 12 was missing because Judas Iscariot had betrayed Jesus and then went and hanged himself.

Since there were meant to be 12 apostles of Christ, and Judas was out, the 11 decided they should choose one more to join them while they were waiting. The two men suggested for the open position were Matthias and Joseph, a.k.a. Barsabbas a.k.a. Justus a.k.a. B-Diddy. We'll just refer to him as Barsabbas.[5] The 11 apostles all prayed about it and then cast lots to pick the next apostle. The Bible says, "The lot fell to Matthias; so he was added to the 11apostles."[6] It was kind of the worst game show ever.

Tonight on "Apostle Pick!" Matthias vs. Barsabbas! Two worthy opponents. One open position. Find out what happens when people pray and then flip a coin!

I'm sure there are a few online comment sections filled with debates over the decision to choose Matthias over Barsabbas and how it all happened, but many people think the apostles jumped the gun and should have waited for the Holy Spirit before moving forward in selecting the next apostle. Whether the apostles did everything right or not, I think the outcome of the decision could have been a bit tough for Barsabbas to hear. According to the little information we have in the text, Matthias and Barsabbas were both qualified candidates. Neither was the obvious pick to join the apostles. Barsabbas had likely given up his day-to-day life to follow Jesus. He'd likely seen the miracles of Jesus and heard his teachings firsthand. Yet, the dice didn't roll in his favor, and that was it.

We don't know much about Barsabbas, but we do know he never revolted against the apostles. He never became a snare in their ministry or went and started a whole new group of evangelists. He didn't take half the congregation and form another church. He never rounded up his other friends and formed another band. Like the *Jew Fighters. Foster the Gentiles. Third Eye Blind Healed. BC Talk. Judea and the Blowfish.*

I've got more of these.

Nothing is ever mentioned about Barsabbas pitching a fit and becoming a barrier for the apostles. This is a story we quickly skim past, but I think it speaks very highly of Barsabbas to be able to accept his place in the ministry of the early church and to move forward in pursuit of the collective group. He saw the bigger mission, and he knew there were greater matters at hand to worry about than a title for himself. Upon finding out he had not been chosen, my guess is he was a bit disappointed, watched the Susan Boyle audition, and then got over it and went on to do great things for the Lord. Christian tradition says he was martyred for Jesus. One of the 12 apostles or not, he was exactly who he needed to be.

God's plans are bigger than ours. Our perceived limitations may actually be God's divine redirection leading us to what he really wants us to be investing in. Do you see yourself as being overlooked or rejected? Or do you trust God is good enough at his job to have you right where you need to be? We have a choice in how we react and in how we view what unfolds in our lives.

I wish I could say that whenever I am overlooked, I lift my head toward the heavens and proclaim, "Not my will, but yours, Lord. You know best. Selah." It usually takes me longer to comply with God. Then in hindsight, I realize I should have just trusted him to begin with.

As we've talked about, I wasn't exactly crushing it after college. During that time, a lot of my prayers went like, "Alright, now what, God? What am I supposed to be doing? I'm still here waiting. Just let me know when you want me to get off the bench. Also, they have 2-for-1 hotdogs at the concession stand. That's a deal even if you don't eat the second one."

During this period, I met a man named Robert Valdez at a church prayer service one night. I knew who he was from a few short interactions here and there, but had never had a conversation with him. I was playing in the band and saw him standing in the very back of the room. I put my guitar down, walked off stage, and walked up to him and said, "I think the Holy Spirit wants us to pray together." He laughed agreeably, and we spent a few minutes praying together.

There are some wonderful moments in my walk with God where I absolutely know something was right, or it's blessed. This was a blessed moment because something supernatural happened in that moment, and Robert and I connected during our prayer together. We exchanged numbers and decided to grab dinner in the next few days. The first of many dinners we'd have together.

At dinner, Robert told me he had spent some time in prison a few years earlier. That's actually how he ended up in Gainesville. He'd accepted Christ while in prison at one of the weekly chapel services. God rocked his world and changed everything about who he was and where his life was headed.

Guardrails.

There is a term called "recidivism" which refers to a convicted criminal's relapse into crime, and it often occurs shortly after they have served time. Within three years of being released, almost 68% of former prisoners are arrested again.[7] So the odds were not in Robert's favor when he was released from prison.

In fact, Robert did end up back in prison, but this time he was the one doing the preaching. God had changed his life so radically that not only was he not another statistic of recidivism, he was now actively engaged in helping other men not become a statistic themselves through the power of the Gospel. He went into prisons all over North Central

Florida on a weekly basis leading church services, and he also worked with a halfway house called House of Hope, which helped men who had recently left prison transition back into society. At our dinners together, Robert would tell me all about what God was doing behind the razorwire and how amazing it was to see broken men finding hope.

When I was growing up, my dad was also involved in prison ministry. I was never able to go with him because I was too young, but I always thought it was pretty cool he was consistently investing in the lives of men and women who were locked away from the world. Also, in my first year out of college, I hosted a Christian radio show on Monday nights. It was an unpaid internship type of thing, and the show consisted of a mix of music, talk segments, and a mini-sermon. One day, I received a letter from a man in prison a few hours south of me. He said he and some other guys would listen to the show every week and would laugh and be encouraged. It was a shock anyone was listening at all, but to know men in a prison located a few hours away were being uplifted was amazing to me. The seeds of prison ministry had been sowed into my life, and I met Robert a few weeks after receiving that letter. Coincidence or God's divine redirection?

I am by no means a theologian, and there are plenty of debates people can have over the Scriptures. But for all of the commentary, I think a pretty easy verse to wrap your head around is when Jesus said, "I was in prison and you came to visit me."[8] Not a lot of room for debate there on what it means. This was the verse that came to mind when Robert invited me to start going with him. So I decided I needed to go and visit some of "the least of these."[9]

True to form, even getting into the prison ministry was difficult for me. For some reason, I had so many issues getting registered and approved to start entering the prisons as a volunteer. I was sent away one morning when I tried to get an

I.D. created at the prison because I was wearing shorts. Who knew that was a rule? Later, I couldn't get an identification number because a clerk had misspelled my name. I never knew it could be so hard to go to prison! I couldn't even get into a place people were trying to get out of.

One morning, after taking time off of work to go attempt to get registered again, I was turned away once more from seeing the prison chaplain because for some unknown reason they didn't have my name on their list. Driving down NW 39th Avenue back to my apartment, I lost it. The culmination of all the other rejection I'd been facing in my life transformed into anger. I was angry at myself and angry with God.

"Screw this, God! I'm done! I'm not trying anymore. You're impossible to work for, do you know that? I thought I was 'called' but I was wrong. You don't want me. You want the sons of pastors who have churches and who get to waltz right into whatever their parents have set up for them. Or you want rich people with connections who can get jobs without trying. Honestly, I don't know what you want, but It's obvious you don't want me. I've been doing everything I know to do, and nothing works, so I'm not trying anything anymore."

I probably should have pulled over for my argument, but I continued to drive, wiping away the tears of my rage and heartache. I texted Robert that once again I couldn't get this prison thing off the ground, and I wouldn't be joining him that evening for service. Or ever. He asked me to meet him that afternoon at a tiny Latin restaurant two blocks from my apartment. I told him about my morning, about my "conversation" with God, and that I was done with everything. Robert sat silently while I finished filling him in and sipped his coffee while looking down at the table. I think he was saddened to hear what I had told him, and there was a bit of awkward silence as he carefully chose his words. Maybe he was making sure he said the right things, or maybe he was listening to the Holy Spirit. We sat in silence for what seemed like an hour but was probably only a few seconds.

"You know that's not God telling you that, right? You know God isn't telling you he doesn't want to use you. When has he ever called you useless? When has he ever said he doesn't want you? Bro, that's a lie from the enemy."

I continued to sit silently. My scrunched-up face of anger slowly turned into a look of surprise as my eyebrows raised a little higher. I honestly didn't have a rebuttal to defend my complaints. I couldn't think of a counterpoint to what he'd said. For once, I was speechless, and the truth rushed over me. All I could say was, "You're right. Wow. I've been believing some big lies."

Robert encouraged me to give it another shot, so I did. I'm not sure why there had to be such a complicated process in the middle of what was already a difficult period of my life when I was only trying to do something good. But within a week, I was able to officially meet with the chaplain of the county prisons, and I began going with Robert on Monday nights. I even fell asleep during my orientation with the chaplain, and they still let me in.

 I didn't know what to expect going into prison. The worst thing on my record was a $76 speeding ticket. My perception of prison was pretty much identical to Prison Mike's from *The Office*, and I was wondering if there were going to be any Dementors flying around. I didn't know if I'd be able to connect with guys who were in there for a variety of crimes.

I was going in to minister to broken men, but I discovered I was also broken in my own way. I needed Jesus just as badly as the men behind bars. There's a strange power in our weaknesses to connect with others who are also weak. It's why we're told in the Bible to "Carry each other's burdens."[10]

We often view that command as, "If you're strong, go pick up the person who is weak," and that's part of it. But as we bear the burdens of others, our brokenness brings us together. We unite in struggle.

At the services, Robert had me lead the worship on the old, busted piano in the chapel, and he even let me preach whatever was on my heart. I shared with the brothers about my own struggles in my faith, my doubts, and my hopes. And there we were, all one in brokenness. We were one in the Body of Christ. Guys would come up to me and tell me they were praying for me, and I told them I was praying for them. Prison was the farthest thing from where I had envisioned my life would go, but it was exactly where I needed to be.

"Then the King will say to those on his right, 'Come, you who are blessed by my Father; take your inheritance, the kingdom prepared for you since the creation of the world. For I was hungry and you gave me something to eat, I was thirsty and you gave me something to drink, I was a stranger and you invited me in, I needed clothes and you clothed me, I was sick and you looked after me, I was in prison and you came to visit me.'

"Then the righteous will answer him, 'Lord, when did we see you hungry and feed you, or thirsty and give you something to drink? When did we see you a stranger and invite you in, or needing clothes and clothe you? When did we see you sick or in prison and go to visit you?'

"The King will reply, 'Truly I tell you, whatever you did for one of the least of these brothers and sisters of mine, you did for me.'"

Matthew 25:34-40

Jesus didn't just say, "I care about the least of these," he went further and said any action toward the marginalized was a direct action unto him. He became weak to make us strong.

Do you feel weak? Jesus is with you.

Do you feel overlooked and forgotten? Jesus is with you.

The truth is, we can all be "the least of these" at some point. I thought I was going to visit broken men, but it only exposed my own brokenness. I needed the same Jesus the prisoners needed.

There aren't any stories in the Bible of Jesus cozying up next to the rulers and the politicians. He was with the outcasts and the forgotten. The overlooked ones who didn't have any hope left. The ones without a plan. The ones standing in distant fields watching sheep while life moved on away from them.

When God closes a door, he's redirecting us for our good, and even for the good of others. Our job isn't to make a name for ourselves and become symbols of status and power. Maybe God will elevate you to a platform with more influence, but it's still not your job to lift up your own name.

Our job is to lift up one Name above all other names. Our job is to lift up Jesus wherever we are.

Chapter 3

Great Mehxpectations

Order Hoarders and Hopeless Warriors

"I'm not fine as in *fine*, but fine as in you don't have to worry about me."[1]

Dr. Greg House, *House*

I think I could write country music. Not because I am an amazing songwriter, I just think I have figured out the formula for writing a hit song. Here it is:

Hit Country Song = (This is stuff I like) + (This is where I'm from)

If you want a super-mega hit, then you would also include stuff about the troops. You think I'm kidding? Have you heard "Chicken Fried" by Zac Brown Band? It was a super-mega hit, and it's just a list of stuff he likes. People go bananas for it. "Yes! I like jeans, too, Zac Brown! He so gets me."[2]

Sadly, I don't think I'll ever write country music. If I wrote a song about what I liked it would be:

I love when my fingernails are freshly clipped.
I love having a full tank of gas.
I love buy-one-get-one free deals on soap.

Actually, that could turn out to be a country hit. That's good stuff. It's not that weird when you consider Julie Andrews' favorite things were bright copper kettles and doorbells.[3] I mean, I love my frying pan, but I'm not singing about it.

I recently realized the majority of my favorite things have a lot to do with stocking up or emptying out. I love when I can get great deals and store up as much of a product as I can. Places like Costco are quite dangerous for me. I'm like a domestic squirrel hiding away laundry detergent for the long winter. Because we're living in a material world, and I am a domestic squirrel.

I also love a nicely vacuumed house or when the garbage is picked up and we are rid of it all. Maybe that's why I loved the garbagemen coming by when I was a kid. Oh wow, it's all starting to make sense now.

I'm not entirely sure why I like stocking up and clearing out so much, but I think it has to do with having control in my life. I don't think I'm a control freak, but I like knowing things are in order. I like knowing if I run out of soap in the middle of my shower I have more in reserve thanks to the BOGO deals. I like having a charged phone and a full tank of gas in case there is an emergency. I never was a Boy Scout, but I still adopted their motto: "Be prepared!"

The older I get, the more I like having routines and specific places to keep my belongings. Part of it is my particular preferences, the other part is, I'll forget about a lot of stuff without a routine. I like having my coffee prepared and set to brew on a timer so I know it'll be ready for me when I wake up in the morning. I like knowing my car keys will be right next to the front door, unless my wife moves them and then forgets where she moved them to and then gets mad when I assume she was the one who moved them, even though I know exactly where I put them because I do it all the time, hence the issue I'm writing about right now.

There are many day-to-day matters we can keep a tight hold on, but in the grand scheme of life, there is actually very little we are able to control. Maybe the Boy Scout motto should more accurately say, "Be prepared for what you can prepare for, but don't think too hard about it because life is nuts. And if you stay in this program too long, then also be prepared to go to prom by yourself."

I've come to hate being asked the questions, "Where do you want to be in five years?" and "What is your career goal?" If I could answer honestly, I'd say, "I have no idea, but I plan to have a lot of soap stocked up under my sink." Don't get me wrong, it's great to have some direction, but life is a continual cycle of our plans falling through. As I look back on the plans I've had, I'm so glad many of them failed. I'm glad I didn't get what I wanted.

I'm glad I didn't marry her. I'm glad I wasn't offered that job. I'm glad I wasn't given that opportunity when I had that mindset, I would have failed miserably. I'm glad I never started watching *Lost*.

Oddly enough, it's hard to accept that we're not super-geniuses who can predict the future, even though we are constantly proven wrong about everything. We want to believe we're carving out our own path with our hard work and superior intellect. The truth is, we can plan as much as we want to, but we're still going to end up making things up as we go along.

No matter how many coupons we collect and how much we map everything out, we're kind of lost and hopeless.

◆ ◆ ◆

Have you ever seen that TV show *Hoarders*?

I definitely haven't. I can barely make it through the previews. It's a show about people who cannot let go of even their tiniest possessions, and they end up living in a house full of junk and filth. Piles and piles of literal garbage fill their houses, requiring a serious intervention.

As I said, I love when the garbage is picked up, so even the idea of hoarding anything stresses me out more than I can bear. They shouldn't ever let me work on a show like that because every episode would be me walking up to the houses, putting on Aviator sunglasses, looking at the camera and saying, "Burn it down. All of it. Let's go . . . Nobody touch me."

And maybe you're thinking, "Hey, didn't you just say how much you love stocking up on soap?" Well, that's different. That's not me hoarding. That's me being a prepared Boy Scout. I just need to know I have the soap and the soap is there for me and . . .

Oh crap, am I a hoarder?

I guess in one way or another we're all hoarders of some sort. We may not have mountains of magazines stacked in our living room, but we hoard other forms of what brings us comfort.

Maybe you just can't get rid of your secret stash of chocolates. Maybe it's the guy you can't stop texting even though it's leading nowhere. Maybe it's the savings account you check multiple times a day. Maybe you can't bring yourself to move from your hometown because of all the relationships and routines you've accumulated there. Maybe it's the "Glory Days" like Bruce Springsteen sang about. Reliving the old memories of the good times of your youth because you can't find happiness in where your life is now.

Hoarding is a sickness, and we don't really want to be cured. It's often the unhealthiest things that bring us the most comfort. But it is counterfeit comfort. (You should probably read Tim Keller's book *Counterfeit Gods*; he wrote about this idea much more eloquently and intelligently.)

For me, eating ice cream is a great boost when I'm feeling sad. The sugar hits quickly, giving me a feeling of happiness and gratification. Then, after I've eaten half the carton, I am more upset than I was to begin with because I am now just as sad as I was and also feel gross. Counterfeit comforts are wonderful in the moment, and they do their work quickly, but they have no positive lasting effects. The lasting effects are the negative ones, like my belly sticking out like *Winnie the Pooh*.

There are so many forms of counterfeit comforts. Binging Netflix for a weekend is a great distraction, but then you start Monday back at work and realize you've accomplished absolutely nothing. Getting drunk is a quick-fix for a night, but you wake up with your problems, and most likely the new problem of being painfully hungover. Casual sex is awesome while it's happening, and then it's over and you're still lonely. Even sex inside of marriage can be a frivolous escape.

If you take part in most actions offering immediate comfort, you can be sure you will not fix the problem and will most likely just wind up with more issues than before. I think if we look deep enough we all realize this. We might even know it before we engage in the actions, so why do we do them anyway?

Probably because it's easy and we're pretty weak. Most temptations don't require hard work. The hardest part of gluttony is getting the wrapping off the food. The hardest part of binging Netflix is remembering your mom's password. Sometimes we don't realize we're addicts, and that's a problem, but often we *do* realize we are addicts, yet we don't take the steps to break the addiction. Being cured means something will have to change. Being cured requires work.

We hoard counterfeit comforts because they give us a feeling of control, but again, it's only a false sense of control. We're not really controlling anything.

In the book of Matthew, Jesus confronted some Pharisees and called them out on their hypocrisy, in a section commonly referred to as "The Seven Woes." He blasted the teachers of the law for speaking one thing but doing another. They would chastise the Jews for not adhering to the Law of Moses, yet they were more steeped in sin than anyone.

> *"Woe to you, teachers of the law and Pharisees, you hypocrites! You are like whitewashed tombs, which look beautiful on the outside but on the inside are full of the bones of the dead and everything unclean. In the same way, on the outside you appear to people as righteous but on the inside you are full of hypocrisy and wickedness."*

Matthew 23:27

The Pharisees enjoyed walking around acting like they had it all together. They loved the praise of people, and they were experts in the Law, quick to instruct and condemn others. Like that one mom at the PTA meeting no one can stand. *Shut up, Karen! You organized the last bake sale and we barely raised enough money to cover the cost of the poster board signs!* The Pharisees gave off the image of having it all together, but in their hearts, they were farther away from God than the prostitutes and thieves. They thought they were in control, but it was only counterfeit control.

Alright look, I am embarrassed at how many times I reference *Jurassic Park* in my life, but here we go again. There is a scene in the movie where Ellie Sattler is talking with John

41

Hammond, Jurassic Park's creator, after the power in the park had gone out and the dinosaurs are eating everyone. He talks about his failure with this park, but says he is going to try it again if he can just regain control. Sattler quickly responds, "You never had control! That's the illusion!"[4] Hammond had deluded himself into thinking it was a great idea to bring dinosaurs out of extinction, and many others joined him in the idea, thinking they had power and control. And yet look what happened. Newman ruined everything, a couple dudes got eaten, and they realized how very little control they actually possessed over the dinosaurs.

We all struggle with John Hammond's same illusion of control. If we can just try a little harder then we'll get it covered. We've got it managed, and we can quit any time we want. *Don't worry, the dinosaurs are safely contained.* We hoard the counterfeit comforts and the illusions of power, when in reality, we have very little control, and we're about to be eaten by a dinosaur.

No matter how on top of the world we feel at one moment, life finds a way[5] to remind us of where we actually stand, and how small we really are. In one way or another, we're all a few steps away from turning on the Susan Boyle video and having a good cry at our desks.

Again, you should just read Tim Keller's book. Though, as good as it is, he doesn't have any *Jurassic Park* references, so what does that tell you?

♦ ♦ ♦

I can't prove it, but I think my wife may have gotten some advice before we started dating to lower her expectations. It's not terrible advice, and it worked out pretty well for me. I think we can apply lowering our expectations to most other areas of life, too.

Your kid made you breakfast for your birthday? Lower your expectations. Have a New Year's Resolution to lose weight? Lower your expectations. Going to see the new *Transformers* movie? Maybe just go ahead and beat your expectations to death.

Part of my struggle with being in control is the expectation that things will work out perfectly, like how I thought my chandelier installation would be easy. Why wouldn't it be? I'd never, ever done anything like it before, so naturally it should go flawlessly, right? What a dumb expectation. Perhaps all expectations we put on ourselves and others are, in a sense, dumb. Someone tell Charles Dickens he needs to change the title of his book to *Meh Expectations*. Or *Mehxpectations* if he wanted to save space.

We all have our moments. I'm sure we've all seen someone lose their mind at a restaurant because the waitress brought them a salad when they ordered a soup. Or we've seen someone flip out in line at Target because the cashier making minimum wage can't find the barcode on a product. It's pathetic. Many of us are so tightly wound, we're like ticking time bombs of entitlement. Life is messy, and things rarely go according to plan. Perfection isn't practical, and everything running smoothly doesn't make for a very good Ben Stiller movie.

Why are we so tightly wound? The short answer is that we all have pride. The idea that we know better than someone else, or even that we know better than God.

The antidote to the disease of pride is humility, and it's a daily medication. Humility means we have to let go. "Letting it go" is an easy concept, and it makes for a great song parents across the world still can't get out of their heads, but letting go also requires some effort because we're so wired to fight for the control.

There is a story in 2 Chronicles 25 about a king named Amaziah. The entire land of Israel had split into two kingdoms; the northern kingdom kept the name Israel while the southern kingdom was called Judah. Amaziah became king of Judah when he was 25 years old, and he was actually a pretty decent one, considering all the horrible kings they'd had in their history.

King Amaziah was going to war against the army of Edom, so he rallied together all of the fighting men he had in Judah, which amounted to about 300,000. In addition, he hired 100,000 men from the northern kingdom of Israel to fight with them. It's kind of odd he could just hire soldiers, isn't it? I've worked with a few temp agencies, but none were for mercenary positions, mostly just editing Microsoft Word docs. Anyway, the king had 400,000 men ready to go do some damage to the Edomites.

Note to self: Develop a Bible gummy snack called the Eat-em-ites. "When you are as hungry as an army, devour some Eat-Em-Ites!" Market them to Christian bookstores and The 700 Club viewers.

A prophet of God stepped in and said to Amaziah, "You can't take the men from Israel into battle with you. The Lord is not with them, and if you go fight with them you'll lose, because God has the power to help you or overthrow you." Amaziah responded, like I probably would have, and said, "Well, I already paid for them, so that would be a complete waste of money! Can I at least get store credit?" The prophet replied, "The Lord can give you much more than that."[6]

Amaziah listened to the word from God and sent the hired Israelite men away, which made them furious. Apparently, the bros were already in their *Tapout* shirts, crushing some Red Bulls, and ready to go throw down. So Amaziah took his original army of Judah into battle and won, exactly as the prophet had told him he would. His obedience to the Lord led to victory.

This would be a great story of faith if it ended there, but the disease of pride infected King Amaziah. Instead of the men dumping a bucket of Gatorade on his head and moving on, Amaziah collected the phony gods of the Edomites and started to bow down and worship them. He even burned sacrifices to them.

Needless to say, God was not happy. As Amaziah was worshiping the false gods, God even gave him a chance to stop by sending another prophet to him who said, "Why do you consult the people's gods, which could not save their own people from your hand?"[7] Amaziah cut him off mid-sentence and said, "Who made you an advisor to the king? Stop or I will kill you."

Blinded by his pride, Amaziah didn't listen to the new warning and kept doing whatever he wanted. He then arrogantly challenged Israel to war. The Israelite bros, who had pent up battle energy and an axe to grind, easily defeated Amaziah's army.

Amaziah's obedience had just led to a miraculous victory, but his disobedience led to his demise. Before he became a winner, he was humble and willing to listen to advice. Then, after he won a victory in war, which God had given to him, he was arrogant and hungry for glory. His counterfeit comfort was his arrogance and the idea that he was a victorious king. In all actuality, his big win wasn't accomplished by his own doing, all he had done was watch God pull off a miracle for the army of Judah.

Like many stories in the Old Testament, I get annoyed with how stupid the people of God were. All Amaziah had to do was listen to God and shut up, but he totally wrecked what could have been an amazing life in service to God and his kingdom. As annoying as it is to read stories like this, the truth is we are probably more like Amaziah than we want to admit. I know I am.

Like Amaziah, we love to take credit for the good things in our lives. Our bank accounts are full because we're such hard workers and fiscally savvy. Our children are at the top of the class because we're parents who truly know how to invest in young minds. Our church is growing because we're relevant to culture, with awesome sermon series like "Fifty Shades of Grace," or "Blessed World." (Say that second one out loud until it clicks for you.) It's easy to take the credit when we have what we want.

But when we don't have what we want, well, that's because the world is cruel. We're in debt because the system is rigged against us and we never had financial support from our parents. We lost our job because HR departments are the worst and never know what is actually going on in their own companies. We're out of shape because eating healthy is expensive and Wendy's keeps mailing us coupons. (These are just a few totally random examples I somehow came up with off the top of my head.)

There may be some truth in all of the reasons we list, for both the good and the bad outcomes. Maybe you really are a great parent, and maybe you were unfairly terminated at your company. However, it's funny how quick we are to accept the accolades but how slow we are to accept any blame for undesirable outcomes.

We promote our successes and proclaim, "I built it myself! Look at the work of my hands! I'm in control of the dinosaurs!" Yet, in our failures, we cry, "Where is God? Why would he do this to me?" We demand perfection in an imperfect world. It's an unrealistic goal, a *mehxpectation*, and a self-destructive way of living.

♦♦♦

King Amaziah never got his life on track after his failure. Personally, I don't think God was finished with him, but he wouldn't let go of his pride. God always accepts humility. In fact, the Bible tells us, "God opposes the proud but shows favor to the humble."[8] God forgave King David after he committed adultery and then repented. God saved the entire land of Nineveh when Jonah preached to them and they humbled themselves, and that was even after Jonah had run away and been given a second chance himself. God doesn't give up on us easily.

We turn into Amaziah when we slide into the driver's seat of our lives. While it is good to have ambition and a strong work ethic, we want to believe we can grab control of our destinies. But ultimately, we have very little say over where we're headed. Who is in control when your kid gets sick? What about when the board makes an uninformed decision and you are laid off? Or when you've done all you know to do and she just won't love you back?

In those moments when we can't change our circumstances no matter what we do, we realize the illusion of control we are under—a *Jurassic Park* revelation. Anyone can be confident after a win, but we find out the truth about our confidence when we lose.

Every Sunday at my church we have a special time of prayer after the message. Our pastor will invite anyone forward who would like prayer for any number of reasons. Maybe they are struggling with family issues or are in need of a divine healing. Maybe there is no specific reason other than just wanting someone to pray for them. We have a prayer team who will go around and lay a hand on a shoulder and pray for each person, and they share what they feel the Holy Spirit is leading them to pray. It's pretty awesome, and it encourages and edifies the church. I wholeheartedly believe God is willing to use ordinary people if we are willing to listen; he did it all the time in the Bible. We are specifically told to pray for one another in the book of James.[9]

One Sunday I decided to go up for prayer. Nothing specific was on my mind or heart, I was simply open to what God would say. My friend Aaron came up beside me, put a hand on my shoulder, and began to pray to himself silently. After a few moments he said, "I have a picture of you in my mind, and you're standing on a hill ready for battle. You have a huge sword in your hand, and you're ready to take on the enemy." I thought, *Nice. I'm a warrior. Am I Brad Pitt in Troy or am I more like Mel Gibson in* Braveheart? *Probably a little of both, and better looking.* Then, Aaron continued, "But there's an enemy army on another hill across from you, and they all have bows and arrows. So you don't have the right weapon for the fight."

Well, that deflated me. I was thinking, *Isn't this supposed to be encouraging? What are you doing? Are you also going to tell me I'm short and ugly, too?* Luckily, Aaron continued, "But the message is that it's not your job to fight the battle. It's God's job. God is the one who will bring victory. It's not about what you can do yourself."

I started chuckling to myself. It was absolutely a word from God for me. A message like that is always relevant to my daily life, but specifically at that moment in time, I had been wondering if I'd done enough for God with my life. Had I worked hard enough? Had I put in enough effort for God to be pleased with me? I wondered if I had somehow missed God's calling at some point in my past because I didn't pray or work hard enough.

The Holy Spirit was reminding me that it wasn't my job to be in control. At that time, I had been trying to make my last book successful and make my career successful, and neither felt successful to me. Honestly, I just wanted to know

I mattered and was doing work that mattered. I was putting my hope in my efforts, and those efforts were supposed to result in accomplishments and a sense of purpose.

We can do all the right things and work harder than ever and sometimes it's still not enough. When we come up short, it's a reminder of our lack of control. We all battle the diseases of pride and control. Enough is never enough when we're relying on ourselves. Without trying to sound religiously simplistic, the remedy is humbly handing over control of our lives to God. The remedy isn't easy because we're not meant to pull it off alone. We have to continually lean on God, and the more we remind ourselves what our job is and what God's job is, and daily let him do his job, things will get better. I would even suggest writing down a prayer and saying it every morning.

Our routines will get altered. Our preparations will let us down. We are all just lost and hopeless warriors standing in battle with the wrong weapons.

But it's not our battle to fight. It's God's. It's time to let go of control, or the illusion of control, and let God be God.

What have we been hoarding? It's time to let it go. What counterfeit comfort do we keep running to for a quick fix? It's time to move on.

Let go of your expectations and let God lead you.

What is your job? What is God's job?

Hey. How are you doing so far? I want to make sure you make it through the book, so I've included this free Zen Garden with each copy purchased. What can I say? I'm a giver.

<u>Free Zen Garden</u>

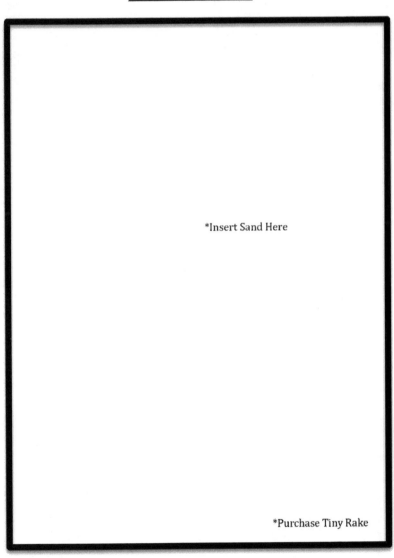

*Insert Sand Here

*Purchase Tiny Rake

Chapter 4

Waiting

Patience is a Virtue and a Huge Pain in the Butt

"I can't give up on stuff. I still want Nickelodeon to take over my school."[1]

Kimmy, *The Unbreakable Kimmy Schmidt*

As I write this book, some of my friends have been trying to get pregnant for the past few months and have been unsuccessful so far. I've been praying for them to get what they want and for God to give them peace. They feel like they are supposed to be parents, and both have a strong desire for children, yet they haven't been able to partake in the journey of parenthood. It's a strange kind of torment.

The desire for children is a God-given one. God told Adam and Eve to have kids right in the beginning. While some people may want to have children for the wrong reasons, and let's be honest, many people probably shouldn't be having children, this longing is ingrained in us by the Father. He's created us with natural instincts and predispositions. You don't have to teach a baby how to eat. You don't have to teach anyone how to sleep. You don't have to teach a girl how to completely break down a boy's will to live. I remember being nervous around girls even in kindergarten. No one had yet told me, "There's a reason girls make you nervous. It's because they hold your soul in their hands, and they will completely destroy you whenever they feel like it. But don't worry, it'll only feel like this for the rest of your life."

As we age and our bodies and minds develop, we become exposed to latent desires and fears that were hiding dormant inside of us, like a hibernating bear we didn't know was in the cave of our minds. The bear comes out one spring day and says, "Hey, the single life was fun and all, but you now want to settle down, get married, and start a family. Also . . . Donald Trump is President? *The Apprentice* guy? Wow. I didn't see that one coming."

I often wonder, if God gives us a variety of innate desires, like parenthood, why would he withhold the fulfilment of those desires from us? Is God sitting in Heaven laughing at us as we run around chasing dreams we'll never catch?

As we discussed in the previous chapter, we all have ambitions and longings. We encourage each other to pursue them, but we often fail to realize that when we chase dreams, some of them may never be fulfilled. As I read the Bible, though, I find this is quite common—the feelings of inadequacy and incompletion. Confusion and anger. Frustration and hopelessness. It's all in there.

In the book of 1 Samuel, there is the story of a righteous woman named Hannah. Her husband, Elkanah, loved her very much, but Hannah was unable to have children. She would continually pray year after year for God to give her children, but nothing changed, and she remained barren and waiting. Meanwhile, Elkanah had another wife, and she was apparently popping out kids faster than Tyler Perry pops out new movies.

The wife who was able to have children would torment Hannah about it. Like when Karen brags about her kids who aren't even that smart and everyone knows it. Hannah would get so distraught over it all that she couldn't even eat. She didn't even have the Susan Boyle video to help her cope. As she grieved, her husband would try to comfort her with sweet and understanding words like, "Hannah, why are you weeping? Don't I mean more to you than ten sons?"[2] Smooth, bro. I assume this was the starting point for many of their couples therapy sessions. "Hey girl, why do you want anything besides me? Look how awesome I am!"

Hannah had a God-given desire she was unable to fulfill. In fact, the Bible goes so far as to specifically say the Lord had closed her womb.

I know. That part is hard to read. Why would God withhold a blessing from her like that? Why would he create within her a hunger he wouldn't satisfy?

Do you have a desire you can't explain? An unfulfilled dream? A missing piece in your soul you can't quite put your finger on? Do you feel like your prayers have gone nowhere? Do you ever wonder if God cares enough about you to actually change anything in your life?

You are not alone. This has been going on for ages.

Feeling abandoned and forgotten by God is such a common biblical theme that even Jesus cried out on the cross, "My God, my God, why have you forsaken me?"[3] And he was quoting a psalm King David had written hundreds of years earlier.[4] The prophet Jeremiah even wrote in Lamentations 3, "[God] has walled me in so I cannot escape; he has weighed me down with chains. Even when I call out or cry for help, he shuts out my prayer, he has barred my way with blocks of stone; he has made my paths crooked."[5]

It's easy to get angry at God over our outcomes. One thought I've always wrestled with is not so much a disbelief in God, but a belief in an almighty God who chooses not to reach into my situations and change anything. A God who will seemingly press the "close door" button of an elevator while I'm trying to get on. In my anger and confusion, I start feeling like God is a bully. If God loves us so much, why is he so withholding?

We don't have all the answers for why bad things happen. We can formulate theological responses, but when you are dealing with an unfulfilled, instinctual desire, or in the midst of a painful experience, sometimes honest answers aren't enough to calm the chaos inside of your heart.

◆ ◆ ◆

At some point or another we all hit our breaking points—a moment where you do what you wouldn't normally do because of stress, fear, or a desperate need for change. It could be difficult to try and name off the top of your head what your breaking points are because they sneak up on you. When you instinctively react, you then realize, "Oh, I guess that's where I draw the line." I'll tell you about one of my breaking points.

Home ownership is great, but I didn't realize when you buy a home you end up with two home addresses. The first is where you sleep, the second is where you actually live—a Lowe's Home Improvement store. If you're currently considering buying a house, take some advice from me and get one as close as you can to a Lowe's or Home Depot. It'll save you hours of driving. Thankfully, our home is only two miles away because we go constantly.

One day, Brittany and I were leaving Lowe's for the 9,000th time that week. Their parking lot has a weird three-way-stop intersection before you turn onto the highway, but the traffic coming from the highway into the parking lot doesn't have a stop sign. I pulled to a stop, looked around for other cars, didn't see any, and began to pull forward toward the highway. As I moved into the intersection, a lady came flying by me from off the highway, I slammed on my brakes, and she promptly flicked me off and pointed to my stop sign while yelling, "You have to stop!"

I don't really suffer from road rage, and I rarely use my horn unless it's to prevent an accident. I like to give people the benefit of the doubt, since I know we all make mistakes. But if someone is knowingly endangering the life of my family or friends by being an idiot, I have been known to lose it. The hibernating bear has shown me how protective I am.

After a moment of shock, I hit my breaking point, said, "Are you kidding me?" and began to drive after her car to hunt her down in the parking lot. I didn't really have a plan, but I was mad and was going to at least say something. Maybe run her over if I needed to really get my point across. You know, for dramatic effect. As I started picking up speed, Brittany braced herself by putting her right hand on the passenger door and grabbing my arm with her left hand while she yelled, "It's not worth it!"

I slammed on the brakes for now the second time in 15 seconds, slowly pulled into the back of the parking lot, and sat in an open space for a moment to calm down. I watched the devil woman get out of her stupid car and walk her stupid self into the stupid store never to be stupid seen again. I assumed she went inside, grabbed a cart, and then proceeded to crash it into the gas grills. I looked over at Brittany and said, "I'm sorry. She was just so wrong!" Brittany said, "Yeah, she was, but it's not worth getting shot over." Fair enough. I admitted she was right, and then I went home and ate some ice cream in silence while I sat on the couch.

You can judge me all you want right now, but I know you have a breaking point, too. Maybe it's not as trivial as a middle finger after someone almost plows into you, but we all have moments where our current temperaments change on the spot. We think we have self-control and patience, but all of our neatly drawn boundary lines go to crap when we are pressured. These are the moments when we find out what's really inside of us.

You laugh at fad diets until you don't like what you see in the mirror one day, and then you Google, "What was that one diet Oprah was doing in 1994?" You swear you'll never let your kids be on an iPad at the dinner table until you want just three minutes of peace, and then you shove Angry Birds in their face. You laugh at online dating until you've been single long enough, and then you're on EHarmony, Tinder, and WillingToSettle.com.

There is another person from the Old Testament who had an experience of questioning God and hit a breaking point. Naaman was a highly respected commander of the army of the king of Aram. He contracted leprosy, a deadly disease for which there was no cure. Lepers would slowly dissolve and then be pushed to the outskirts of town, unable to come in contact with everyone else. They were sent away to die alone as outcasts.

Naaman had a servant girl who had heard of Elisha, the prophet of God, and she suggested they go see him. Naaman had no other option but to go. He had wealth and honor among the people, but none of it could save him. He was at his breaking point. He showed up at the house of Elisha with horses, chariots, and loads of silver.

It's funny how Naaman was dying a gruesome death, yet he showed up with pomp and flair, trying to act like he had it all together. We do the same thing. Life is a wreck, but we can't let on to others that we don't have it together or else we'll look weak. So we post a picture on social media of us doing something fun or intellectual with just the right filter. I assume, just like Naaman, we're not fooling anyone.

> *Elisha sent a messenger to say to him, "Go, wash yourself seven times in the Jordan, and your flesh will be restored and you will be cleansed."*
>
> *But Naaman went away angry and said, "I thought that he would surely come out to me and stand and call on the name of the Lord his God, wave his hand over the spot and cure me of my leprosy. Are not Abana and Pharpar, the rivers of Damascus, better than all the waters of Israel? Couldn't I wash in them and be cleansed?" So he turned and went off in a rage.*

2 Kings 5:10-12

I wish I didn't relate so much to Naaman, but I probably would have had the exact same reaction. When I need something from the Lord, I read my Bible, and it says stuff like, "Wait on the Lord,"[6] "Trust in him,"[7] and, "Put your hope in the Lord."[8] Then I get upset because it's not the answer I want, and I don't see immediate changes. I start to debate with God and think I know more than he does. It's the pride issue we talked about before. It's a battle between my desire to follow God and my desire for comfort. Like Hannah, sometimes we even have good desires, yet they are unfulfilled.

Why wouldn't God just allow Naaman to be healed by the word of the Lord, or at least give a more practical command? That would have been easy for God. Why would God specifically close Hannah's womb when he designed her to be a mother?

It's frustrating to read these stories, but we need to stop and think about how God could have kept details like these out of the Scriptures. He could have said, "Actually, that point makes me look mean and withholding. Let's change the Instagram filter." Yet, it's all clearly written in there. God wants these hard-to-swallow details to be in the Bible. He wants us to know Hannah was upset, yet he wasn't changing her situation. In fact, he seemed to be working against her.

We are allowed to question God, but nowhere in the Bible does God ever tell us we'll get the answers we want. In fact, he says, "As the heavens are higher than the earth, so are my ways higher than your ways and my thoughts than your thoughts."[9] There are many different reasons and greater purposes for why God does what he does beyond what we can figure out. Naaman couldn't understand why Elisha would say his cure would come by washing in the Jordan River, but he reluctantly decided to try it when he'd hit his breaking point. He went to the Jordan River, dipped himself seven times, and then he was miraculously healed.

I think I know what is best for me, yet as time moves forward, it proves I am consistently wrong. It's the war of our own desires fighting against the plans of God.

In the Chronicles of Narnia book *The Silver Chair*, there is a group following the orders of the mighty king Aslan the lion. They are sent to awaken another king who is frozen in time on a silver chair. After they finally find him, they are debating whether or not to actually go through with what they were told to do. They were afraid the frozen king would immediately kill them. As they are debating potential outcomes of their actions, the character Puddleglum finally speaks up and says, "Aslan didn't tell [us] what would happen. He only told [us] what to do. That fellow will be the death of us once he's up, I shouldn't wonder. But that doesn't let us off following the signs."[10] That moment is a great snapshot of what it's like to follow God. We don't really get to know where we're headed, we just know we're supposed to follow him. (Spoiler alert: The king didn't kill them. I know you were worried.)

Our breaking points force us to let go of our control, give up on our abilities, and lean completely on the Lord. But when we run to his arms, we are always met with grace. We aren't condemned, we are restored. God is ahead of our story with open arms just waiting for us to catch up.

◆ ◆ ◆

There was once an ancient text that could be found inside thousands of churches and homes not too long ago. It was a mysterious book called a "hymnal," and it contained hundreds of songs written over the years by Christians. I know, it sounds crazy, right? Read out of a book while we sing? Why not just look at the lyrics on a screen? Well, some time ago, churches didn't have lyrics on a screen. They didn't even have coffee at church. This was a dark period in church history we don't like to talk about. That period was roughly the last 2,000 years up until 2009.

Hymnals are the Blockbuster Video of churches, meaning if you see one nowadays, you're probably in the middle of nowhere and someone is about to murder you. You may recognize some hymns as Chris Tomlin songs, but that's a common misconception. He just writes new choruses for a lot of them. Like many children, I grew up singing hymns. They were great because they had some history to them and weren't put out as quickly as Hillsong albums are now— which is every two weeks. Those are Tyler Perry numbers right there. Hymns were rich in theology, and most contained an evil "Verse 3" we all had to skip over to save time during worship sets. I still enjoy hearing many of them today. They will pop into my head at random moments, too.

Recently, the hymn "Alas, and Did My Savior Bleed" came to my mind. It's commonly referred to as "At the Cross." Also, I literally just Googled "at the cross" to make sure I would be quoting the exact lyrics, and Chris Tomlin's song "At the Cross" was the first thing to pop up. Can't make this stuff up. Anyway, here are the real lyrics to its chorus:

At the cross, at the cross where I first saw the light,
And the burden of my heart rolled away,
It was there by faith I received my sight,
And now I am happy all the day!

Ironically enough, the original lyrics to this song were written by Isaac Watts in the early 1700s, and then this chorus was added by Ralph E. Hudson in 1885. I guess Hudson was the original Tomlin.

As I was thinking about these hymn lyrics, I found the last line of the chorus a bit unsettling. "Now I am happy all the day." I'm not sure how accurate that is to our faith in Christ. I don't think it's worth burning hymnals over. I'd even be fine with singing this song at church, but only if Chris Tomlin adds a second chorus to it and we skip the third verse. However, I do believe it contains a misconception about walking with Christ. The truth is, we're often not happy all the day. Some days we are even the complete opposite of happy.

If we were to rewrite this lyric, it could maybe go something like, *"Some days I'm happy but many days I am just clinging to the hope that God will turn my sorrow into joy and if he doesn't at least I know all things will be made new one day and there will be no more of this crappy suffering in eternity but until I get there I will try and not depress everyone with my bleak outlook because melancholy people don't get invited to a lot of parties."* I guess it's a little long for a hymn, but it's more theologically sound.

Life isn't easy when we are waiting on a miracle, an answer, or even peace. The Bible says, "In bitterness of soul Hannah wept much and prayed to the Lord."[11] As she clung to the goodness and mercy of God, she wasn't happy all the day. She was praying in her heart passionately and mouthing the words silently. The priest Eli thought she was drunk at the temple of God. He told her she should stop drinking, and she replied, "I am a woman who is deeply troubled. I have not been drinking wine or beer; I was pouring out my soul to the Lord."[12]

It's easy to read the Bible and think it's just names and stories, but these were very real people with very real lives and issues. We're not distant from the same emotions, questions, and pain.

At first glance, this story seems to be about a woman being tortured or ignored by God, but that would be because we didn't know where the story is going. Hannah is about to give birth to a boy named Samuel. Samuel will go on to become one of the greatest men to ever live. A mighty priest who will lead Israel, speak the words of the Lord, and who will even anoint the shepherd David as king. Hannah was not waiting on and praying for an ordinary boy.

It's impossible to know where our stories are going, but maybe when we feel like God has hit the pause button on our lives, it's because we're not just waiting on a simple blessing. Maybe God is up to something bigger, beyond our scope of imagination and understanding. I don't mean to simplify prayer or give false promises of waiting and benefits of enduring pain, but I hope we realize we're not the experts of timelines. I hope we believe God is for us, not against us, no matter how things may look in the moment.

I mentioned Pastor Carl Thompson earlier in this book. You've likely never heard of him, but to me he is one of the greatest men to have ever lived. We need heroes, and he's one of mine.

He was the pastor I had for most of my adolescence in Ocala, FL, and he'd known me since I was born. We used to go to lunch with his family most Sundays after church, and we spent a lot of Christmases with them as well. When I moved from Ocala to go to college in Gainesville, about an hour or so north, I would drive down and see him every so often. We'd sit in his office for hours and I would bring my questions I'd gathered over the weeks from my conversations and Bible studies. He would answer them all in grace and wisdom, and we'd talk about life in general. I enjoyed it immensely, and I believe he did, too.

Pastor Thompson had to be put on daily kidney dialysis during the last years of his life. It was a painful and tedious process, and not what you'd want to see anyone you love have to endure. Through it all, he kept preaching and pastoring his church, loving his wife and family, and surprisingly to me, he was never angry with God.

One Sunday evening, I decided to go visit my old church and see him. It was one of the only churches still doing Sunday night services, so the crowd was sparse. But I just enjoyed being back in the old pews I used to crawl under and sleep on. After the service had let out, he said, "Jonathan, do you have a little time to grab a bite to eat?" I obviously couldn't turn that invitation down. It was a Sunday night in Ocala, which meant the options were very limited. So we went to Wendy's on Highway 441. Truth be told, we probably would have picked Wendy's no matter what else was open because we weren't sellouts. And Wendy's has been there for me almost as much as Pastor Thompson.

We ordered hamburgers and fries and sat down at a little two-seat table by the window. We talked about our lives, family stuff, faith, and the ministry. I was about 24 years old at the time and unsure where things were headed for me. I was wrestling through what I discussed with you in Chapter 2, wondering what God had for me. Here I was, sitting with a godly man who had devoted his entire life to the Gospel.

A man who, at 76, had followed through on his decision to follow Jesus in the good times and bad times. Now he was a man who was suffering as his body was failing him, and his God wasn't healing him.

I asked him point blank, "Aren't you upset? You've spent your entire life devoted to the ministry, and now you've been suffering through all of the dialysis. Don't you want to know why this is happening? What do you say to God?"

He didn't even pause to think his answer through. "I don't need to understand. I just need to serve him."

I've never forgotten those exact words. It was how a man of God answers. A man who had walked with God way longer than I had and who had his feet planted on the Solid Rock. A man who had seen the light at the cross, and the burden of his heart really had rolled away. I don't mean to glorify him and act like he never sinned or doubted God. He was a human, and he had his struggles and shortcomings just like the rest of us. But at the center of it all, beyond emotions and fears, his faith was set on the hope of Jesus Christ, and his name was written in eternity.

He didn't have to think through an answer to give, because the Answer was alive inside of him.

The strength and humility I saw in him became a life goal for me. We hugged goodbye, and that was the last time I saw him on this side of eternity.

He was never divinely healed. Within a year of our conversation, he was on his deathbed in a hospice facility, and I was living up in Washington D.C. Never once did he shake and deny God. He left behind a powerful legacy of faith, and I believe his prayers are still at work today in the lives of the many people he poured his heart into. I am just one of the many.

When suffering comes into our lives, we can know God is not wasting our time, and it somehow even brings us closer to God. Something is happening in our hearts.

The prophet Jeremiah of the Old Testament is known as "the weeping prophet." We read one of his laments earlier in the chapter. It's believed he was the primary author of the Book of Lamentations. He was likely lamenting over the fall of Jerusalem and the lack of repentance among the Israelites. In Lamentations 3, he wrote about a personal torment of his soul. Jeremiah was fighting for hope through the pain.

I remember my affliction and my wandering, the bitterness and the gall.

I well remember them, and my soul is downcast within me.

Yet this I call to mind and therefore I have hope:

Because of the Lord's great love we are not consumed, for his compassions never fail.

They are new every morning; great is your faithfulness.

I say to myself, "The Lord is my portion; therefore I will wait for him."

The Lord is good to those whose hope is in him, to the one who seeks him;

It is good to wait quietly for the salvation of the Lord.

Lamentations 3:19-26

I love this passage because Jeremiah is living in the real world, and he wasn't delusional enough to say, "Everything sucks around me, but it's cool because I am happy all the day!" He said, "I acknowledge the grief and pain and torment, yet I will set my mind on the Lord's love." This kind of reaction is our only hope in the waiting and pain. What God is producing in us and through us will be greater than the pain we endure. It's actually a lot like childbirth.[13]

We don't need to understand. We just need to serve him.

♦ ♦ ♦

Eugene Peterson said in his book, *Run with the Horses*, "When we are born, we are named, not numbered. The name is that part of speech by which we are recognized as a person; we are not classified as a species of animal. We are not labelled as a compound of chemicals. We are not assessed for our economic potential and given a cash value. We are named. Names not only address what we are, they also anticipate what we become. Names call us to become who we will be. A name calls us to become what we are not yet."[14]

I recently did some number crunching and discovered an interesting stat. Roughly 87% of the people in my life are named Mike. I know. It's crazy. I assume the stats are probably similar for you, too, and I found out why. According to the Social Security Administration,[15] from 1954-1998 the most popular name for a boy was Michael. Except in 1960 when it was second place, for nearly 44 consecutive years Michael dominated the charts, proving Americans know a good thing when they see one, and being creative is exhausting.

Michael is a solid name, but I'm not sure why it was so popular for 44 years. Nowadays, we give our children names because of what the name means to us, or who it honors and stuff like that. However, back in Bible times, many of the names given to people were very symbolic. Moses means "Drawn from the water," because the Egyptian princess drew him out of the water. Names would also seem to prophetically speak over what the child would go on to be like. Jacob means "Supplanter" or "to trip up." Just ask Essau if he lived up to that name. David means "beloved" and everyone loved him (except Saul). The name Jonathan means "Gift of God." Well, I'd say that one is spot on. Also, you're welcome.

Early the next morning they arose and worshiped before the Lord and then went back to their home at Ramah. Elkanah made love to his wife Hannah, and the Lord remembered her. So in the course of time Hannah became pregnant and gave birth to a son. She named him Samuel, saying, "Because I asked the Lord for him."

1 Samuel 1:19-20

The name Samuel means "asked of God" or "heard by God." He was a gift to Hannah and a gift to Israel, as he led the people of God for decades. He lived a righteous life until the day he died.

Hannah, the woman who couldn't fulfill the desires of her heart, finally gave birth to a miracle. The Bible says, "The Lord remembered her," but that doesn't mean he'd ever forgotten about her. In fact, she was always known and loved by God. The name Hannah means "favor and grace." Her name spoke the truth over her life that she was favored by God, even when she felt like she was forgotten. The whole time she was barren, she was still favored. The whole time she suffered, she was in the grace of God. She was never out of God's sight or plan.

◆ ◆ ◆

Oh, by the way, about that couple from the beginning of the chapter. At the time I finished writing this chapter, they found out they were pregnant with a boy. I wonder what they'll name him.

Chapter 5

Come Fail Away

The Measure of Success

David Wallace: "What do you think are your greatest strengths as a manager?"

Michael Scott: "Why don't I tell you what my greatest weaknesses are? I work too hard. I care too much. And sometimes I can be too invested in my job."

David Wallace: "Okay. And your strengths?"

Michael Scott: "Well, my weaknesses are actually . . . strengths."[1]

The Office

When I was around 15 years old, my mom made me go see a doctor for a routine checkup. She just wanted to make sure I was healthy and there were no major issues we were missing. Nothing sounds like more fun to a teenager than needlessly going to the doctor, getting half-naked, and sitting on the thinnest sheet of paper ever made. I figured after seeing the doctor, maybe I could write a book report just for the fun of it, too. Then how about flossing my teeth for a few hours?

The doctor was a very tall and thin man. He resembled Ichabod Crane from the old Disney cartoon *The Adventures of Ichabod and Mr. Toad*. He was very serious and didn't really have great bedside manner. (Is it still called "bedside manner" when you're just sitting on a table in your underwear?) He never even made eye contact with me or tried to be conversational. As we wrapped up the exam, he asked, "Are there any specific health issues you are experiencing?" I jokingly said, "Nothing really, except that I'd like to be taller." He turned and looked at me, in all seriousness, and said, "Okay."

Apparently, my joke delivery needed some work. I did a half chuckle with an awkward smirk. My mom knew I was joking, but she didn't laugh out loud for some reason; I thought it was pretty solid material. None of this mattered because I had lit the fuse of inquiry and Dr. House was on the case. He started asking me questions about when I stopped growing and what my diet was like. I didn't know how to respond. I told him I was only kidding, but he didn't care and ignored everything I said. He left and came back with some brochures for me to look at and some pills to take. I felt like Jack who had just gotten some magic beans. Thus, I learned that unless you're speaking with Patch Adams, it's probably best not to make jokes with doctors, especially ones who look like Disney characters. Just remember that in case Dr. W. T. Pooh ever meets with you.

Maybe I should have taken the pills. After all, no one has ever had to ask me to duck down at a concert so they can see the stage. The truth was that I felt like I was just running a little behind my peers. I was waiting for the legendary growth spurt to kick in. I wanted to play basketball but knew there could only be one Muggsy Bogues in the world. Most of my friends had hit puberty and grown a few inches in height over the previous years. I kept thinking I'd be next in line, but I never did get that sweet growth spurt. Honestly, I'm still not sure if I ever hit puberty. At what age does it technically change from "acne" to "adult acne"? And when does your voice stop sounding like a Muppet?

I think life is full of moments where we ask ourselves, "Am I getting anywhere? Does any of this effort matter? What is the point? Am I even growing?"

At my current job, I have to pull a lot of reports of quarterly stats and create graphs and pie charts. I've actually been dubbed the "King of Graphs" by my coworkers. So, in your face, girls from my high school who thought I wasn't boyfriend material. Every metric from my daily work activities is measured and analyzed, but it's hard to do that with the rest of our lives. I can't exactly plot my entire life into a flow chart of character growth over the last 10 years. There aren't any reportable metrics for life's progress. You can't create a PowerPoint presentation about how close you've gotten to God in the last quarter or pull a report on how your giving specifically impacted third world countries. The worst anniversary gift would be to give your spouse a Microsoft Excel sheet full of stats about your investment into your marriage and where you have room for growth in the next fiscal year. I'm sure some data nerd out there is thinking, "Actually, that's not a bad idea." Trust me, it is, and that's coming from the King of Graphs.

Since we struggle to see growth in our lives, we end up asking, "Am I just wasting my time and energy?" We sit around waiting for growth spurts to kick in. We can consistently do what we know to do but still fail to see the difference it's making. Since we struggle to measure our growth and progress, we place standards on ourselves that are impossible to live up to. We chase after dreams we think will make our lives count for something. We work toward ideas of success and meaning we've developed based off of what we've seen in our friends' lives on social media. These are loosely defined goals, and if we ever even reach them, they usually don't live up to the hype.

We are not the first people to feel this way or ask these questions. The Apostle Paul told the Galatians, "Let us not become weary in doing good, for at the proper time we will reap a harvest if we do not give up."[2] I think Paul knew better than anyone about giving your life to something and wondering if it was worth it. I'm sure he had those questions pop up whenever he was being beaten for preaching about Jesus. Yet, he reminds us not to give up on what we know we're supposed to be doing, and that all the effort means something and is going somewhere, even if you feel like you're only sitting around waiting for a growth spurt.

Fortunately for you, your life is not like my height. You are getting somewhere, and what you are doing matters. Also, unlike me, you probably aren't in your thirties and still being asked "What grade are you in?" by the leaders at a youth group event. (True story.)

◆ ◆ ◆

I grew up in church, so getting married was the ultimate goal of life. If you shared a similar background as me, you probably felt like life wouldn't really begin until you had a sweet ring on your left hand. It was a weird retelling of *Lord of the Rings* where all of us in youth group were Gollum wanting "the precious." I heard so many people say, "God told me I'm going to marry them." It was a convenient way of saying, "I am so not their type, but I'm not crazy for having a huge crush on them." Apparently, God is a terrible matchmaker because none of the people I heard say that ended up marrying each other.

Around this time, the book *I Kissed Dating Goodbye* got really popular. It basically said no one should date until you're already married or something like that. Author Joshua Harris has since apologized for his approach to dating and marriage, and I wouldn't ever put the entire blame on him for the issues over marriage in church youth groups. But we all had a crazy idea that marriage was the Promised Land, and if you were married, that meant you suddenly had your life together. However, the divorce rates in the church have continually proven otherwise.

Maybe my next book should be called *I Awkwardly Kissed Dating: God Told Me You're Going to Marry Me*. With chapter titles like: "Missionary dating," "We're not dating, we're just talking," "Don't tell the youth pastor I'm going to prom," and "I'm dating myself right now."

My parents didn't have a picture-perfect marriage and ended up divorcing while I was in college. The parents of many other friends I grew up with in church ended up divorcing as well. Surprisingly, it didn't give me a fear of marriage; it actually gave me a determination to do it better. I gave myself the challenge to do things differently than my parents did. I placed upon myself an impossible standard to live up to, and I had no way of measuring my progress. No pie chart or X and Y axis could report my growth towards this fantastical goal. All I really had was a mental list I'd created of Do's and Don'ts. *Okay, my parents did* this, *I won't do* that. *My dad didn't do* this, *so I will do* that. Like any idealistic young adult, I let my pride tell me I would do it better.

When we attempt stuff like that, we end up finding out pretty quickly how we are just as human as everyone else. What are our measuring metrics? How do we know we're accomplishing these impossible goals? We compare ourselves to others, or we compare ourselves to ourselves. Those are both formulas that lead to disaster. We'll discuss this a little more in the next chapter.

When Brittany and I got married, I was 28 years old. I wasn't some dumb 19-year-old. I had life experience and character building years. Therefore, I was a dumb 28-year-old with impossible, self-imposed standards to live up to.

I'd been in serious relationships before, but no amount of experience or marital counseling can prepare you for how things actually play out in a loving, committed marriage. Nothing preps you for sharing a bank account and having to justify your Amazon purchases to someone else. I also found out that in the middle of an argument it doesn't do much good to use the excuse, "Well, I didn't handle that the way my parents did, so at least I'm not that bad." That means nothing to someone who didn't grow up in your home. *Actually, maybe some graphs and pie charts would help me better emphasize my point . . . No. No, that's stupid. Come on, King of Graphs, you're better than this!*

Marriage forces you to confront the issues and proclivities you've kept hidden in the cave with the hibernating bear. You're not just a roommate with someone, now you've become one with another person. They will get to know you in a way no one else ever has, and you will also get to know yourself in a way you never have. So it can get ugly.

A big goal of mine within marriage is to never have a temper. As you already know from my chandelier story, I've failed in that goal. I was a fairly quiet kid growing up until I came out of my shell in late middle school. But deep inside my growth-stunted body, I hid some monstrous rage. I definitely remember when I was very young how I didn't like being picked on or made to feel like I didn't belong. For example, whenever my sister's teasing went too far, the rage would come out. I would transform into the Incredible Hulk, except I was very small and not green. Although I *did* have purple sweatpants on because it was the early 90s and you could dress like that. I didn't like feeling inadequate, and I still don't today.

Some people who know me nowadays probably think I'm a Type A person. I can be an organizer for events. I've realized many people won't plan any kind of get-together because they are sooooo popular that they are the ones always being asked to hang out. Well, I've accepted the role of being an initiator, and initiating is a Type A thing to do. I just accept it. Still, others who know me think I'm a Type B. I'm pretty laid back and generally an upbeat kind of guy. I'm naturally more passive than aggressive. However, I've realized they would both be correct. I am Type A or Type B depending on the situation I am in.

Maybe you fluctuate between these personality types as well. In fact, life often requires us to alternate between the two at any given moment. You can't remain completely mellow if your house is on fire, and God knows we need Type A people to actually get stuff done. *Braveheart* would have been an entirely different story if William Wallace was Type B. "I guess we should, like, do something about the oppression? I dunno. Maybe we're overreacting out here with the face paint." But you can't be so high strung that someone getting your order wrong at Burger King makes you flip out. "I paid for large fries, you goon! Burn it down! Burn down this kingdom of burgers! They may take our fries, but they will never take our freedom!" The unrealistic goal I have for myself is to maintain a perfect balance of these two personality types and remain even-keeled at all times. Unfortunately, especially for my wife, I haven't mastered this yet.

One beautiful day a few years ago, Brittany and I decided to ride our beach cruisers around Jacksonville Beach. There are a few picturesque streets that run along the beach. The traffic is slow and sparse, and there are always people out enjoying the day. We'd been married around two years at this point. We went through a lot in our first few years together because we were both unemployed at different points, changed a couple jobs, moved three times, and bought a house. So on this day, I was genuinely happy and amazed we were biking around together in our new world that finally seemed to be settling down from all the changes.

We were leisurely biking through the streets, and it was all so nice that I assumed we were about to break out into song like the von Trapp children. I started to head from the road to the sidewalk. Unfortunately, Brittany wasn't paying attention and collided into me on her bike. She knocked me into the sidewalk curb, and as it was happening, I yelled, "Watch where you're going!"

This is one of those moments I've discovered in relationships where what happens next can either diffuse the tension or completely blow it up into a massive war. What starts as an insignificant miscommunication can be peacefully settled or become the triggering point for a battle royale. Your near future hangs on the next few seconds after the moment of impact. These kinds of instances happen constantly in relationships. So naturally, being the peacemaker that I am, I immediately cooled the tension by apologizing.

False. I made it all worse.

After I yelled what I did, which I didn't think was out of anger but just a reaction to being hit, Brittany got mad at me for yelling. I didn't think I had actually yelled at her, so I decided to really just light the whole situation on fire and said, "You were about to run into me. Did you want me to whisper, 'Pssst. Hey, sweetie, could you not slam into me?' What did you expect me to do?" It was a terribly stupid answer. It didn't diffuse the tension and, unsurprisingly, made it worse than it needed to be. We got into a fight about God-knows-what from there. I honestly don't even remember because it was such a dumb fight.

And, of course, our friends Phil and Leigh just happened to be biking by at that exact moment and stopped to say hi.

This always happens when Brittany and I are fighting. We're always about to meet up with friends or go into church, and then we have to pull it together and act like we don't despise each other and instead are out loving life and taking awesome pictures for Instagram. I'm pretty sure Phil and Leigh picked up on the uncomfortableness of it all, so they cut the conversation short and politely biked off, and I'm sure they were judging our marriage for having any lowpoints. They *do* have a perfect marriage; I know because I've seen their Instagram accounts.[4]

Brittany and I decided to keep biking, but we weren't really talking at this point. If we did talk, we were passive aggressive or snarky. Fighting while being on a beach cruiser is like going to a funeral without pants on. It's depressing, and you feel ridiculous. "I'm so sorry for your loss. Also, can you turn the heat up a bit in here? It's getting a little chilly."

Biking in silence gave me time to think. I realized at this point I was no longer mad at the actual altercation, I was mad at myself for sucking so much as a husband. Kind of the same way I got mad at myself during the chandelier ordeal. I was mad I had failed my wife and my marriage so badly. Why couldn't I have been calm and collected? Why couldn't I have just lost that fight? Why couldn't our marriage be like all the others on Instagram? Why couldn't I have been a perfect husband like Phil? I got angrier with myself than I ever was at Brittany. I'm my own worst enemy.

Also bees hate me.

So myself and bees are my worst enemies.

We eventually parked our bikes by the Ocean Rescue tower in Atlantic Beach and walked down to the shore. I began to address the situation between the two of us as we'd had some time to cool off by then.

After apologizing for whatever the heck had just happened between us, I said, "I'm a bad husband."

Brittany kindly responded, "No, you're not a bad husband."

"I think I am. I'm a bad husband."

"You really aren't."

"No, I am. I'm a bad husband. And I think I have to accept that. I am a bad husband because it's impossible to be perfect all the time. I want to be perfect, and then when I'm not, I get angry at myself. I need to accept that I'm a bad husband. It relieves the unnecessary pressure to be someone I can't ever be."

I didn't realize it in the moment, but I was tapping into the revelation of what Paul wrote about in 2 Corinthians.

[God] said to me, "My grace is sufficient for you, for my power is made perfect in weakness." Therefore I will boast all the more gladly about my weaknesses, so that Christ's power may rest on me. That is why, for Christ's sake, I delight in weaknesses, in insults, in hardships, in persecutions, in difficulties. For when I am weak, then I am strong.

2 Corinthians 12:9-10

We're big on knowing our strengths, but we have to recognize our weaknesses, too. Our weaknesses are embarrassing, but they are open doors to the power and grace of God. We should absolutely acknowledge our weaknesses. Paul even went as far as to say he delights in them. That's a crazy idea, but the weaker we let ourselves be, the stronger we actually become. Remember that at your next job interview when someone asks you what your greatest weaknesses are.

"Oh boy, I'm glad you asked about my greatest weaknesses! I delight in them! I am closed-minded, constantly late, and most days I have no clue what I'm doing. Isn't God so good?"

"Interesting. And your strengths?"

"I'm the King of Graphs, baby."

If we can learn to accept the reality of God's grace in our weaknesses, we can then learn to give ourselves grace, too. We can let go of the pointless pursuit of perfectionism and grow spiritually, emotionally, and relationally. That's why Paul delighted in acknowledging his weaknesses.

We often spot our weaknesses and become insecure about what we are lacking. However, boasting in our weaknesses will turn insecurity into confidence because weaknesses mean we have no other option than to rest on Christ's power. We won't feel the weight of thinking everything we strive for in our lives depends on our own abilities. With God, our weaknesses are actually good news. That's how overwhelming his grace is.

♦ ♦ ♦

"Put your money where your mouth is!" Not only has this phrase been used countless times in 90s sitcoms, but it's also one of the worst pieces of advice you can give anyone. Firstly, putting money in your mouth was a *no-no* I learned at a very young age while trying to show my mom how many pennies I could fit into my cheeks. Secondly, it's the beginning of a wager that usually doesn't end up going well for the person it's being said to. Zack Morris knows what I'm talking about.

In one way or another, we all come across moments where we have to put our money where our mouths are. We have to stand by what we've said we believe. If we're right, we look smart and confident. If we're wrong, maybe we'll change our opinion. Or we might be so thick-headed that we stick with our views no matter how much evidence is given to us. Like when will you people ever quit with this whole "Earth is round" idea? Have you ever seen a map of the world? The map is clearly flat. Quit fighting science!

Oh, the thrill of being right about something you've wagered! It's intoxicating. It's a rush of joy and relief. I recently had this rush when I figured out how to set up sprinklers in my lawn where the water spray would reach just far enough to water the edge of my grass, but not so far to where I would be getting water on my neighbor's fence. Brittany and I were driving to dinner on the day I figured it out, and she said, "You look happy. What's up?" I continued looking confidently ahead at the road and replied, "I was nervous I wouldn't be able to actually do it, but I figured out how to get the sprinklers on a timer and to cover the entire lawn, and it actually worked." "Oh. Well . . . that's good," she said, looking somewhat confused.

If you're reading this in your twenties, this sounds ridiculous. If you're reading this in your thirties or older, I know you get it. You totally get it.

Taking a risk is terrifying. When you're young and free, taking risks is exciting because the worst-case scenario is moving back in with your parents, and free meals and free WiFi are not a bad fallback plan. However, as you get older you have more to lose, so you're less inclined to be a risk taker. The shame or embarrassment will stick with you longer, too, as the decisions and failures have greater, more impactful consequences. As a result of a failed risk, you may have to change where you live or change where you work. Or if you were a Jewish fisherman around the year A.D. 30, you may have your failure written down for millions of people to read for the next 2,000 years. But that's the worst-case scenario.

The Apostle Peter is one of my favorite people from the Bible, as he is to many others. I think we love him because we relate to him so easily. He was a well-intentioned, passionate man who stuck his foot in his mouth a lot. It's easy for people like me to identify with that kind of person. We love Jesus and we want to do the right thing, but we're kind of like a toddler who is stumbling everywhere with very little control.

By the 14th chapter of the Gospel of Matthew, Peter had been walking around with Jesus and seeing miracles with his own eyes; he was even a part of miracles, like when Jesus calmed the wind and the waves. He'd witnessed the Messiah raise dead children to life, heal the blind and lame, cast out demons, and feed thousands of people with just a few loaves of bread and some fish. I got excited about sprinklers, so Peter must have really been in awe. Peter was physically walking with God, and there were no limits anymore. The impossible had become possible. No more constraints from the laws of physics. And perhaps best of all: unlimited breadsticks.

After the feeding of the 5,000, Jesus told the disciples to get into their boat and "go on ahead of him to the other side while he dismissed the crowd,"[5] which I assume meant he was signing autographs and doing interviews with the media. "Yeah, you know, we just tried our best out there. Wanted to give the crowd 110%. I have an awesome team with me, and we just, you know, we work hard, and I think it's gonna be a great season." Jesus never gave the disciples further instructions, just like we mentioned in the last chapter when Puddleglum tells the Narnia kids that Aslan didn't give a full set of instructions. The disciples were floating in a boat on a lake without their leader as the night got later and later. They didn't really know how Jesus was going to catch back up with them.

All of a sudden, in the middle of the night, the disciples saw Jesus approaching their boat by walking on the water. As we all would have been, they were afraid, and some thought they were seeing a ghost. "What do you want from us, apparition? We'll give you Judas! He's the best of us. Here, we'll throw him overboard for you."

But Jesus immediately said to them: "Take courage! It is I. Don't be afraid."

"Lord, if it's you," Peter replied, "tell me to come to you on the water."

"Come," he said.

Then Peter got down out of the boat, walked on the water and came toward Jesus. But when he saw the wind, he was afraid and, beginning to sink, cried out, "Lord, save me!"

Immediately Jesus reached out his hand and caught him. "You of little faith," he said, "why did you doubt?"

And when they climbed into the boat, the wind died down. Then those who were in the boat worshiped him, saying, "Truly you are the Son of God."

Matthew 14: 27-33

I'm a child of the American church, and as such, I've been to many church retreats, conferences, and camps. There's a term in Christian circles called "youth camp high," which means when students return from a retreat, they tend to be very focused and engaged in their church and youth group. They sing passionately during the worship services, many times flooding the front few rows of the service. They are reading their Bibles at night and committed to seeing a change in their schools. Then after a few weeks, the adrenaline fades and things go back to normal. The battle every youth pastor faces after a retreat is to try and keep the fire burning.

We all experience the youth camp high in some way or another. Maybe we just had a great vacation with our family, or our spouse has suddenly started paying more attention to us, or we finally got the promotion we've been wanting at work. Or maybe we successfully set up sprinklers in the front yard. We're flooded with excitement, but as with all things, it slowly fades away, and everything becomes normal again.

So Peter, too, was experiencing a youth camp high the night Jesus walked out to them on the water. Remember, he'd witnessed all the miracles of Jesus with his own eyes, and he'd just seen 5,000 people get fed with a few snacks. So when he saw Jesus walking on water, maybe he was carbo-loading from all the bread, or maybe he truly believed anything was possible. He believed in the power of God and took a bold step of faith. But just like Peter, as we take steps of faith, sometimes we may start looking at the wind and the waves around us and end up wondering what we were thinking when we got out of the boat. We start to feel unprepared, unqualified, and scared. The high we were feeling starts to fade, and we find ourselves drowning in anxiety, shame, guilt, and insecurity.

We wonder if we're getting anywhere in life. Are we growing spiritually? Are we improving? When is the growth spurt coming? Are we just destined to drown?

As Peter began to drown, Jesus reached out his hand and caught him. When we read the words Jesus said next, it's easy to read them as direct and harsh. "You of little faith; why did you doubt?"[6] That can be read as, "Come on, dummy. We've been through this before." However, I don't think Jesus was chastising Peter here. I think he was encouraging him as he was pulling him up out of the water. The Bible says Jesus was impressed with the faith of certain people in various stories,[7] so it's likely that Jesus was amazed by Peter's faith to even get out of the boat and do something no one else had ever done. When he said, "Why did you doubt?" I believe he was saying it with a tone of love and encouragement. The Lord is patient with us[8] and slow to anger.[9] He sees us for who we are in him, not who we are when we are drowning.

Jesus uses our failures to work good in us. Our weaknesses allow us to rely on his strength. If we walk with him, our failures don't have to pile up into a mountain of shame we carry with us. Little by little, failure by failure, we are actually progressing and growing as we learn.

If we learn something from it, then failure isn't failure—it's an education.

I think Brittany would tell you I've gotten progressively better in my reactions. Some of it came from self-realization after the chandelier and beach biking incidents. I've learned to accept that I can't keep things perfect. Trucks get scratched. Carpets get stained. Brand new blenders shatter when your wife leaves a spoon in it and turns it on. Again, these are just random examples I'm pulling out of the air, not things that occur on a regular basis in my home.

I'm still imperfect, but she accepts me as her husband even in my imperfection, and I accept her in her imperfections. I can only truly accept her if I accept myself, and I can only accept myself by trusting in the grace and mercy of Christ. I have to know I'm already accepted by the King. I'm loved not because of my works; I'm loved because of his grace.

The only way Peter walked on water was by taking his eyes off of his own feet and locking eyes with the One who created the water. That miracle wasn't important because Jesus was looking for water-walking disciples so they could get rid of using boats, it mattered because Jesus was looking for disciples who would take a step of faith and rely on his strength that is perfect in our weaknesses.

Jesus is still looking for the same kind of disciples today.

Chapter 6

The Thief of Joy

Don't Look at Me Looking at You

"We're very lucky in the band in that we have two visionaries, David and Nigel . . . They're two distinct types of visionaries, it's like fire and ice, basically. I feel my role in the band is to be somewhere in the middle of that, kind of like lukewarm water."[1]

Derek Smalls, *This is Spinal Tap*

I am Princess Jasmine. I am Rey from Star Wars. I am Katniss Everdeen. I am . . . apparently a lot of women.

How do I know I am all of these people? Well, because I've taken internet quizzes telling me so. You've probably taken these same types of quizzes online when you should have been working. Buzzfeed and other sites like it will put out these quizzes for us to find out who we really are. *Which member of the X-Men are you? Which character from Harry Potter are you? Which kid from* Stranger Things *are you?* We've all wasted our time and waded through 12,000 ads just to find out we're Chandler Bing.

Quizzes like these are popular because they are kind of amusing and pointless, but there is also another reason. Even though we know they are cheesy and stupid, we want to believe the best about ourselves. We desire a form of affirmation, distorted as it may be, because we all need the attention and love in one way or another. Even the people who say they don't care what anyone thinks about them want people to care that they don't care about what people think.

A big struggle for me is feeling like I'm lagging behind in the race of life. It's a stupid idea to begin with because if life is a race, then that means the finish line is death. So why am I trying to beat everyone to death?

Note to self: Change the wording in that last sentence during the book editing so I don't sound like a murderer.

I have been "late" to many of life's major events. As you already know, I'm still waiting on that growth spurt, but I was also late to my college life at the University of Florida because I went to community college for my first two years. Then for my first year at UF I commuted from my parents' house an hour away from campus to save money. Starting your college career at a community college is like going to a pool party and swimming in jeans. You're there, but it feels awkward and uncomfortable. So by the time I got to UF and started getting involved in Christian campus organizations, church, and other activity groups, the friend circles of people my age had long been forged. I felt too old to still feel new at a university, like Larry King trying to get onto an Ultimate Frisbee team. Students welcomed me in as I continued showing up to events, but I don't have the memories and inside jokes my friends have from their first three years of college together. Sometimes when we hang out now I still feel like I'm missing out on the memories.

I didn't get married until I was 28. That may not sound old to you, but in the Christian world that feels like decades behind everyone else, like Larry King getting married for the eighth time at age 64. Being single throughout most of my twenties meant there were a lot of lonely nights and long walks home for me. There were awkward blind dates, painful online dating attempts, even some speed dating. I have to say, out of all three of those, speed dating was surprisingly the best. Instead of going back and forth online before you meet in-person only to find out your date is a total weirdo, with speed dating you get to immediately find out they are a weirdo, which is a great time saver. Oddly enough, I'd met my wife Brittany when I was 21 and had a crush on her, but it took her seven years to make up her mind about me. (Even though God told me I was going to marry her . . . Just kidding.)

The most recent area I feel behind in is having children. As of right now, we still don't have kids, and I'm in my thirties. Again, that may not seem old to you if you live in a major, progressive city. But down here in Jacksonville, my church is populating itself faster than a guinea pig love shack. Having kids in your mid-to-late thirties can feel like you're Larry King having kids at 66. (I did way more research on Larry King for this book than I was planning on.) People will often say to me, "There's never a right time to have children," like we should just get it over with already, and then in the next breath they say, "Oh, just wait until you have children! You have no idea how tired and miserable you'll be." That's not a very good sales pitch.

I wish I didn't compare myself to others, but it's hard not to do it, isn't it? I'm sure you have areas you feel like you're behind in. Should I be making more money? Should my home be bigger? Should I be in better shape? Should my life have a little more adventure in it? It's hard not to look at others on social media and wonder if there's something wrong with us because we haven't been able to make life come together as easily as many of our friends are seeming to. What are they doing right that I am not doing? What am I missing? Would I be farther along if I'd spent more time hustling and less time researching Larry King?

Comparison is a double-edged sword. It's the quickest way to make yourself feel behind in life. Alternatively, it's also the quickest way to stir up your pride. You may see yourself as doing better than someone because you are farther along or have achieved more than someone else.

It's dangerous to compare ourselves with others because we are all living in different timelines. We get to some life events earlier than others, and others get to some events earlier than us. That doesn't mean either person is wrong. Sure, sometimes we may have areas where we need to get our act together and we can follow someone else's lead, but if we are seeking the Lord's plan for our lives, we shouldn't be surprised when we see diversity in how those plans play out. God has made us all very different, and we're not all heading toward the same life events or callings. He has a specific timeline for each of us to live in.

◆ ◆ ◆

As we mentioned in Chapter 2, the nation of Israel didn't have a king for a long time. They were led by the judges, prophets, and priests of God, but ultimately, their leader was God. The common way of life for most other nations in the world at that time was to be led by a king. God had a plan for Israel to be different than the other nations—a different timeline for them to live in. He desired for them to be a kingdom of priests and a holy nation.[2] He had delivered them into the Promised Land and given them their own nation, as he had said he would do.

True to human nature, the Israelites said, "Nice idea, God, but even though you performed astounding miracles before our eyes and gave us tons of victories in battles, we think some random dude could lead us better." They said to the priest Samuel, "Appoint a king to lead us, such as all the other nations have."[3] God replied to Samuel, in what seems to be a tone of genuine disappointment, "It is not you they have rejected, but they have rejected me as their king. As they have done from the day I brought them up out of Egypt until this day, forsaking me and serving other gods, so they are doing to you. Now listen to them; but warn them solemnly and let them know what the king who will reign over them will claim as his rights."[4]

Samuel then warned Israel of how a king would take advantage of them and their children and turn them all into his servants. Israel replied, "That's cute, Sam. But uuummm, I *think* we know a little bit more than you do, alright? All we've done since day one is screw everything up for ourselves, but we're going to go with our instincts here. We want a king."

They were acting like a bunch of high school brats who just found Wikipedia and think they know everything. And like the high school guys who act like you don't know how to exercise because you're in your thirties and have love handles. These twerps have 6-pack abs on a diet of Coke and burgers, yet they think it's because they know so much more about fitness than you. It's called "metabolism," dudes, it's on your side right now but it'll turn on you faster than the Israelites turned on God! This is just another random example I'm making up on the spot.

If you read through the Old Testament, you'll find the majority of Israel's kings became a burden to the people. The kings even led them away from God to serve foreign gods, which made life much harder than it needed to be. God had a unique timeline for Israel full of blessing and prosperity, yet they lost out on it by comparing themselves to others. They looked at other nations on Instagram and were deceived by their seemingly perfect photos taken at just the right angle with just the right filter.

I can't fault the Israelites too much because, once again, I do the same thing. The benefits of God aren't good enough for me when I'm focused on what I don't have instead of what I do have. The grass is always greener on the other side, and what you don't have looks a lot more fulfilling than what you currently have. It's like having the latest and greatest smartphone, at least until the day the newer model is released. Suddenly, your current phone becomes an embarrassing metal brick shouting obscenities at you every time you hold it. "You suck! You're so out of touch and old! And your father never loved you!" Old phones can be quite cruel, but it's because they themselves are hurt and crying out for love on the inside.

How many times do we get what we think we want and it's still not enough? How many marriages end in divorce because someone thought marriage would magically make them happy? How many people move from job to job, surprised to find out that work is actually work wherever you go? How many people live under the weight of debt because they thought a few purchases would give them the confidence and status they needed to fit in?

We all feel the need to have something rule and reign as a king in our lives. Just as Israel served its kings, we also serve ours. Our kings give us feelings of security or status for a time, but it's never enough. No matter what we accumulate or what social status we achieve, we will always have that voice in our minds telling us we're still not enough. We need more.

◆ ◆ ◆

Teddy Roosevelt famously said, "Comparison is the thief of joy." He also had the less famous quote, "I hope someone will one day carve my face onto the side of a mountain in the middle of nowhere." Comparison is not only a thief of joy, it is also that friend we all have who leads us into making the dumbest decisions.

In middle school and high school, my best friend (who refuses to let me call him out by name in this book, so we'll just call him "Swiss") always thought it'd be a good idea for our group of guys to end up in our underwear at some point. We'd run through the neighborhood scantily clad just because Swiss said, "You know what would be funny . . . ?" One of my favorite lines of dialogue I have recorded on a home movie is when my friends and I were taping various "stunts" in high school, trying to be like the guys on *Jackass*. Swiss thought it'd be a good idea for us to do stupid stunts like jumping off the roof into a pool and out of trees onto piles of leaves. In the background noise of the tape, you can hear the following dialogue:

"Why do we always have to do what Swiss wants to do?"

"Hey, if we were doing what Swiss wanted to do we'd all be naked."

Comparison is the Swiss of all good decisions; it leads you into stupidity. Nothing can deter a great idea like someone else with another idea. Especially if you want to be liked. I can't tell you how many times I've changed my plans or opinions in the past because I wanted to fit in.

During my sophomore year of high school, I ended up seeing *The Perfect Storm* in theaters twice. I know! It's not even that good of a movie, and it's super depressing. I'd gone one Friday night to see it with my friend Len. The next day some girls from our youth group wanted to go see it. We asked if we could see something else since we'd literally just seen it, but for some reason they really wanted to see George Clooney and Mark Wahlberg on the big screen. So we went again. I had to sit through a movie about sailors drowning twice within 24 hours, and none of the girls even wanted to hold hands. Len and I waved goodbye to them after the movie, feeling like idiots. "Bye, girls! Glad we could be here since your boyfriends didn't want to come! So cool how we can just be friends and you can have absolutely no attraction to me whatsoever . . . God told me I'm going to marry you."

Peer pressure is a term most synonymous with adolescence, but it lasts our entire lives. When you get older it's called "Keeping Up with the Jones'," which means you're trying to stay on par with what your peers have going for them. If you're "Keeping Up with the Kardashians," it means you've lost all sense of dignity. Peer pressure will often cause us to do things we may not have otherwise done, and although a lot of it is petty, sometimes there can be major consequences in bigger matters.

One of the weirdest, Narnia-like stories of the Old Testament is found in the book of Numbers and is about a prophet named Balaam. The country of Moab was an enemy of Israel, and Balaam was commissioned by its king to put a curse on Israel. Many scholars believe Balaam was not actually an Israelite, but kind of a rogue prophet who apparently had a reputation for hearing from God and knowing if disaster was coming, hence the reason the king of Moab thought he might curse Israel for him. He seemed to be in it for the money, so I guess you could also call him a "profiting prophet." Eeeehh? My dad joke game is on point right now. God spoke to Balaam and told him not to curse Israel, and Balaam obeyed the command. Upon hearing of Balaam's refusal of his request, the king had his officials ask Balaam to come to Moab to meet with him. God eventually told Balaam he could go, but strictly said to only do what he commanded.

Soon after, Balaam got on his donkey and joined the king of Moab's officials to go meet with the king, but joining the king's men was in direct contradiction to what God had commanded. This angered God, so an angel of the Lord came and stood in the middle of the road, ready to kill Balaam if he came any closer. Balaam didn't see the angel blocking his path, but his donkey did. So the donkey walked off the road into a field to avoid being struck down by the angel. Balaam beat the donkey and forced it to get back on the path. The angel stood in the way two more times, and the donkey tried to avoid it each time, which infuriated Balaam and caused him to continue beating the donkey.

Then all of a sudden, the Lord enabled the donkey to speak to Balaam and it said, "What have I done to you to make you beat me these three times?" For some reason Balaam didn't think this was weird enough to freak out over or even pause for a moment to consider that an animal was speaking to him. I guess this was just another normal day for him as Dr. Dolittle. He snapped back, "You have made a fool of me! If only I had a sword in my hand, I would kill you right now." The donkey, whom I've decided to name Mr. Stubbornton, replied, "Am I not your own donkey, which you have always ridden to this day? Have I been in the habit of doing this to you?"

Then God opened Balaam's eyes to see he was about two steps away from death. The angel of the Lord told him the donkey he was beating had just saved his life. I bet it was an awkward, quiet ride home, like after mom and dad get in a fight at Chili's.

So Balaam had an actual conversation with his mode of transportation. He was the original *Dashboard Confessional*. This is such an odd story and it's easy to want to call Balaam an idiot, but once again, we're probably more similar to the character in this Bible story than we'd like to admit.

Why did Balaam flip out so easily? Well, for one he was probably a short-fused, arrogant kind of guy. But more than that, he was riding with a king's officials. He had been placed in the company of people who had influence and power, who were decked out in the finest of their king's royal clothes, and who probably also thought very highly of themselves to have the roles they had in their king's service. Balaam was in the company of people who were out of his league. The upper echelon of society. The prestigious kind of socialites who get to go to parties with Weird Al.

It reminds me of when I would go to a happy hour networking event in D.C. while I was unemployed. Everyone who attended always had amazing, important careers, and the first question anyone asks you in D.C. is, "What do you do for a living?" My response was usually, "Oh I work at *[insert the name of the last place I did temp work at, answering phones at the front desk]*."[5] I would make up answers because I didn't want to feel like I didn't belong. It must have been odd when I would immediately follow up my response to where I proudly worked by asking, "So is your company hiring?" Then I'd take the Metro home, depressed and listening to Billy Joel sing, "You had to be a big shot, didn't you?"

So when Mr. Stubbornton started dodging the angel of the Lord, it made Balaam look like he couldn't handle his animal. He looked undignified when he desperately wanted to be considered an equal. He had lost his illusion of control. He was dealing with the same issue we discussed in Chapter 3. We want to be in control, and it's embarrassing when we aren't. So Balaam took it out on the very animal who was saving his life because he wanted to fit in.

I wonder how many times we have an angel in the road who is blocking our plans. I wonder how many times God has said, "No," while we are saying, "Yes." How many times have we been driving toward our own plans when God is stopping us and sparing us from destruction? We pray for God's blessing and plan for our lives, then we get angry when we're not getting what we want. Under society's peer pressure, we try to force ourselves into someone else's timeline when God is trying to keep us in the one he has for us.

We may not be deliberately fighting or rebelling against God, but our human nature is constantly in opposition with his will. Jesus even had to pray, "Not my will, but yours be done."[6] Our desires must become God's desires. If we seek his will, his Spirit will lead us to what will not only be better for us, but will also make us better. God is leading us to eternal treasures and eternal purposes, not just fleeting counterfeit comforts.

I guess I could have gotten married to a couple of women before Brittany, but they weren't the ones for me. If I'd wanted to keep up with my peers, I could have ended up in a terrible marriage. I'm glad there was an angel in the road. That "angel" was me being completely broke and sleeping in bunk beds.

As I said earlier, my wife and I don't have children yet, even though people keep mentioning that we should. To be honest, I play the "numbers game" a lot and try to figure out how old I'll be when my kid is graduating high school. Will I still be able to hear their name announced over the speakers? Will my motorized hoverboard scooter be able to get me up into the stands? I try and figure out how old is too old to be having kids. At what point do perceptions move from "Oh, he's a little older of a dad" to "Holy cow, Larry King just had another kid? Ew." But God hasn't given us the desire yet to move to that stage of life, and no one else should be making these decisions for us. We have to trust God knows what he's doing. I'm not going to beat up on a donkey because I feel a little insecure and behind in this specific race, and it's not really even a race.

In the story of Balaam, it took the most notoriously stubborn animal to call out another stubborn animal. It truly takes one to know one. When it comes to peer pressure, an important thing to remember is most people are idiots. And I say that as an idiot who just happens to recognize his stupidity. So from one stubborn beast to another, I say we strive to trust that our Father knows what he's doing, where he is leading us, and what he is redirecting us away from. Likewise, we can trust that he's not only redirecting us away from what will destroy us, but he is also leading us to what is infinitely better than what we've settled for. He is continually calling us to know him in a deeper way.

The thief comes only to steal and kill and destroy; I have come that they may have life, and have it to the full.

John 10:10

♦ ♦ ♦

Do you ever find yourself repeating the same lines of dialogue in your life? Maybe it's the same story you love telling or the same responses to particular questions. My wife has heard me make the same jokes over and over, and while I'm sure it annoys her, I can't help that it's solid material. But hey, I've heard her go into her own repeated spiel anytime someone asks her about the most important thing in her life—our dog Walter. "We don't really know what his breed is. He's our little rescue buddy! Yadda yadda yadda, I love him more than my husband." She doesn't actually say that last part . . . but she doesn't *not* say it.

One of the most repeated lines of my life comes after people ask me if I've seen a movie. My response is often, "I saw some of it, but I fell asleep during it." Sadly, this isn't a phenomenon that has occurred suddenly in my thirties. I've been falling asleep in movies since I was a kid. My friends even had a running joke in high school that if they put on a movie after 8:00 p.m. then they knew I'd miss it. Needless to say, I never got to pick what movie we watched. I can't help it. I love movies, but I love sleeping more. Have you ever slept? It's amazing.

I've seen the movie *Arrival* twice, and by "seen" I mean "I've started it twice and fell asleep through it twice." From what I can tell, it looks like it's actually a great movie. If you haven't seen it, allow me to spoil it for you with what I remember:

There are opening credits and Amy Adams is in it.

Alien spaceships show up on earth.

Hawkeye from the Avengers comes along.

Octopus looking aliens write stuff on the glass.

Something about a bomb?

The aliens aren't bad like Independence Day aliens, but more like E.T. *aliens who were here to help us.*

End credits.

Pretty great recap, eh? Here's the part that's really stuck with me:

The aliens are communicating with humans through their own writing, which is some kind of circular form; they weren't writing left to right like we do. We then find out the aliens can see into the future and time to them wasn't linear either. They could see into the future and knew they'd need our help one day.

Wait, so the aliens were smart enough to see into the future but not smart enough to figure out how to write in English? Interesting. Maybe that part was explained while I was sleeping.

I don't think aliens will unlock our brains any time soon, but it really made me think about how God sees time. We are moving forward in our linear lives, however fast or slow they feel, and we can only look back on what has been. We look at the timelines of others and feel behind, yet we don't know where or what we're all headed toward.

God doesn't move in our linear timelines. He's outside of time altogether. The Bible repeatedly speaks of God moving outside of our timelines and having his specific plans and purposes laid out before the world was formed.[7] It hurts my brain to think about how that is even possible, but I also like serving a God who is bigger than my understanding. God is big enough to have individual purposes and plans for each of us, and with a God who loves diversity so much, we shouldn't be surprised that we aren't cookie-cutter clones.

I wonder what we're complaining about right now that will work for our good in the future. I wonder what we're confused about right now that will make so much sense when it comes together in a way we never could have expected. I wonder if God is ahead of us in our linear timelines shaking his head, laughing, and saying, "If they only knew where this was going. Also, they are going to be so sad when they find out how many more *Transformers* movies are yet to come."

Psalm 139:5 says, "You go before me and follow me." This verse tells us God is so good that if we are committing our lives to him, he is ahead of us preparing our futures, and he is also behind us cleaning up our mistakes. Who are we to say we know best when we can only see what is behind us and what is directly before us? We're walking on a linear path while God is moving wherever he wants, unbound by time.

Do you remember Hannah from Chapter 4? She was experiencing the pain of a linear timeline. Her heart longed for more while she was mocked for being barren. She prayed to God for a son and waited. She was waiting in her linear timeline, but the entire time Hannah was praying, God knew he was going to give her a son who would become one of the greatest men to ever live. Hannah didn't just receive a new son, she received a new heart.

The modern English spelling of Hannah is a palindrome, which means her name reads the same frontwards as it does backwards. If I'm not reaching too far here, I think it's a beautiful analogy for how God sees our lives. We're judging our lives and results in a linear timeline. We're only reading it in one direction. Yet God knows where we are and where we're going because he's before us and he's following after us. He sees who we were, who we are, and who we will be.

The second chapter of 1 Samuel captures Hannah's prayer of thanksgiving to God. I think it's worth noting that the other wife who was taunting her didn't have any of her prayers written down for millions of people to later highlight in their Bibles. In fact, she's never mentioned beyond being a tormenter.

So Hannah, the woman who wept uncontrollably because she wasn't seeing her heart's desire fulfilled, ended up being the one who wrote, "My heart rejoices in the Lord... My mouth boasts over my enemies, for I delight in your deliverance."[8]

Don't waste your life looking around you. Look upward and put your trust in the eternal, almighty God. Put your hope in the One who goes before and behind us.

Instead of taking Internet quizzes to find out who we are like, we should ask God, "Who did you create me to be?" The God who made us knows exactly who we were meant to be, and we won't look like anyone else. He's too creative of a Creator to repeat himself.

97

So I had this whole thing planned out with a printing company to include an awesome motivational poster with the book. Really encouraging stuff you could put up in your cubicle or bedroom. Then a week before we went to print, they were all like, "Who are you again? We thought you said Jonathan Taylor Thomas. We were so thrilled." So I've had to improvise.

Chapter 7

Hey Jealousy

Or Virtual Insanity or Some Other 90s Pop Song

Liz Lemon: "You're so insecure you get jealous of babies for their soft skin!"
Jenna Maroney: "And how much attention they get."[1]

30 Rock

As I said in the last chapter, my wife has heard me tell the same jokes many times. Well, there's also another anecdote she's heard more times than she can stand, but I can't help if I think it's fascinating. A few years ago, I read *The Birth Order Book* by Dr. Kevin Leman, and now I think I'm Sigmund Freud.

The book discusses being the first born, middle child, youngest, or somewhere in the middle of a big family. Dr. Leman shows stats like how many U.S. Presidents were first-borns or the only child in a family.[2] He talks about how the youngest children have to find their own way to stand out, which means many of your favorite actors and comedians are likely the youngest in their families. And many therapists and guidance counselors are middle children because they are used to being peacemakers or conflict avoiders while the oldest and youngest tend to fight for attention. Or just fight.

I started talking about this book at every party we went to. I was analyzing my friends and people we'd meet. I'd tell everyone where I thought they were in their birth orders, and then they would all bow to my genius.

Actually, I was wrong quite a lot. I was basically a human Magic 8 Ball, just spitting out random guesses. While the tendencies are obviously not 100% accurate for all people, it's still interesting how birth order can often affect our personalities, ambitions, and perspectives.

The Brady Bunch girls are famously one of the best examples of all of this. Marsha was the oldest. She was beautiful and popular with a dry-as-toast personality because she was good looking and didn't have to be even remotely interesting to be loved. Cindy was in her own world of cuteness and weirdness as the youngest. And then, of course, there was the middle child, Jan Brady—television's beloved cynical wet blanket. She was constantly in a state of frustration, self-loathing, and jealousy. I like to think Jan now hosts her own show on a cable news network, entitled *And Them's the Facts with Jan Brady-Matthews*. The most famous line of Jan's existence was an exasperated confession of the jealousy she had for her sister: "Marsha! Marsha! Marsha!"

I give you all of this background information to let you know of a disorder many of us could be diagnosed with. Sadly, you probably haven't realized you have it. I don't mean to ruin your day with my doctoral knowledge, and I hate to be the one to tell you this, but it's likely you have a mild to severe case of JBS. Known more formally in the medical world as *Jan Brady Syndrome*.

I'm sorry. I'll give you a moment to let the news sink in.

In the last chapter, we talked about feeling behind in life and comparing ourselves with others. I probably could have shortened the entire chapter to three words: We are jealous.

When we start comparing ourselves with others and feel like we are missing out, it's likely because we want what others have. Jealousy is such a big deal that God included it in the Ten Commandments, yet it hides itself within us and we don't call it out enough. We probably don't call it out because we don't recognize it. That's why I had to diagnose you with JBS. Now that you know you have it, you can start fighting it.

Some of the many JBS symptoms include gossiping, guilt trips, looking up your friends' houses on Zillow, and saying things like, "Well, that must be nice for them."

This is a hard chapter for me to write because it means diving deep into my sins and insecurities. I'd like to skip this chapter altogether, but you have to have a Chapter 7 to get to Chapter 8, so I can't do anything about it.

♦ ♦ ♦

One of my favorite activities any time I go to New York City in winter months is going to the ice skating rink. Living in Florida doesn't provide you with a lot of opportunities for ice activities other than sticking your face directly into a freezer because it's so hot outside. I never actually ice skate whenever I'm there; I just enjoy people-watching, and by that I mean I like watching people uncontrollably and helplessly fall down. I think it's hysterical. I was in Central Park last December with my friends Mike and Bharath, and I made them stop by the ice skating rink with me, even though they were puzzled why we were doing it. Moments later we were all in tears laughing at the adults and children eating it pretty hard on the ice. I like to think I help my friends see the most beautiful parts of life.

Maybe you think I'm heartless, but it sounds worse than it is. Or maybe I'm just a horrible person. Either option is a possibility. Watching people fall is so funny to me because it shows me we're all really just undignified humans trying to pretend like we have it all together. There is no way to look cool while slipping and landing on your butt.

Beyond ice skating falls, can we all just admit that sometimes it feels really good to watch someone fail? Maybe it's your older brother who was a star in high school yet has been in college for 12 years now while you have a solid career going. Maybe it's when you see a married couple who posts cute pictures all the time on Instagram having a fight in the middle of Target (or fighting while biking around on beach cruisers). Maybe it's finding out the person at your job who always critiques your work is being let go. *Have a nice life, Karen!* If we're being completely honest, sometimes it feels pretty darn good to see someone who is good at a lot of things be bad at something you're good at. Sometimes it feels good to watch our friends fall.

Initially, it's not evil to feel a sense of relief when you watch others not succeed. It can be encouraging to know, "Oh good, it's not just me." But that can easily and quickly cross a line at a certain point and our JBS will flare up.

Where is the line? It's when we start having thoughts like, "At least I'm not *that* bad," and, "I guess they should have done what I did instead." When we think those kinds of thoughts, we begin to cross the line separating empathy from jealousy and pride. Often times, the leap across that line can go completely unnoticed.

Jealousy makes us think someone else's success is getting in the way of our own success. Like there can't be more than one accomplished person in the world, or even in a group of friends. It's easy to think if someone has something you don't have, then you're a loser. The only time someone's success should bother you is if you're competing on *The Voice*.

Jealousy is a liar and a manipulator. It will only ever bring pain and damage into our lives. Life is too short to spend it wishing you had someone else's.

♦ ♦ ♦

Sometimes I wonder if I have a nemesis. Is there someone out there who is competing with me and against me? Is there a Draco Malfoy in my life? There might be. I know I've had at least one.

When I was in middle school, I played point guard on the basketball team at my school. We played against this one team across town a few times a year. Their team had a boy my size as their point guard, so naturally we were matched up against each other every single time. He really was such a Malfoy. He even looked like him. He had blonde hair, his soul was as dark as midnight, and his family was likely rich because he was at a nice private school on the affluent side of town. Whereas, I was at a "private school," but my school's students weren't usually the children of doctors and lawyers; we were the children of pastors, teachers, and horse farmers who just wanted their kids to pray with their teachers before lunch. We were essentially The Mighty Ducks of private Christian schools.

It's funny because Malfoy and I never spoke to each other even once. No one ever said, "Oh, there's your nemesis," but we knew it every time we looked at each other. We'd both think, "Here we are again. Let's do this." And what sucked is his team would always win. However, somewhere there is a video of me pulling a sick crossover on him and driving to the hoop and scoring. I like to think it still keeps him awake at night. And clearly I don't have repressed memories of our rivalry I still can't get over.

So do we actually have a nemesis? The truth is: maybe. They might not have an all-out focus on you and a secret lair where they are actively plotting against you, but I am fairly certain someone is competing with you in some way or another.

How do I know? Well, stop and think. Is there someone who comes to mind right now that you are competing with, even in the slightest of ways? Someone whose Facebook posts make you jealous at times or kind of annoy you? You, of course, click *Like*, but you also think, "Must be nice for them, they never had to *[insert the one random thing in your life that worked against your success that they didn't have to deal with]*." If you can't think of one person, then you make me feel really bad right now because I can think of a few.

Yeah, I hate this chapter. Anyone want to skip ahead to Chapter 8 with me?

Maybe your nemesis consumes your life, but for a lot of us, it's only moments of envy that pop up without us expecting it. We cross that line, jealousy sneaks its way in, and we can end up being jealous of the people we really do love and root for. At any stage of life, the grass is always greener somewhere else, and it's hard not to wish we had what someone else had, even just for a moment. Someone will always have something you want in a variety of areas in life. The danger is when we sit in it and feed the jealousy. As with any sin, it grows if you let it. The more we focus on what we don't have, the more insecure and selfish we become. Jealousy never leads to our benefit in any way.

It's all a bunch of lies and a house of mirrors. You may be jealous of how much money someone has, but they may be jealous of something you have that they don't, like a super awesome homemade sprinkler system. Your nemesis doesn't know you're competing with them, and you don't know who is competing with you. When jealousy grows in us, we think we're in a battle against others, but in reality, it's only a battle within ourselves.

Most of what we see in people's lives, especially on social media, isn't the whole truth. You're seeing their best moments because we can't find filters cool enough to beautify the ugly moments of our daily lives. It's like if someone hadn't heard of Michael Bay and they saw the first *Transformers* movie and thought, "Oh, he's a decent director. That was pretty cool." That's what social media is—the first *Transformers* movie. Our real lives are the sequels where you think, "How could it possibly be this bad?" Then Michael Bay is like, "Hold on, we ain't done yet! Here come 27 more! Each one progressively worse than the last!" What we tend to see about others is merely a highlight reel we can't keep up with because it's not reality. If we were able to see behind the scenes of the social media posts, we'd see some ugly stuff. We'd see life without filters and reshoots.

I've lived long enough to know the people you envy one day can become the ones you pity the next day. I was jealous of people I watched get married while I was single and lonely, only to find out a little while later they were divorcing and going through the hardest time of their lives. There have been esteemed speakers and celebrities I've envied who have ended up in scandals, affairs, and drug addictions that destroyed everything they had worked for. We think we want what they have, but in reality, what they have could bring us to ruin. They are counterfeit comforts that jealousy is lying to us about. What we want so badly could be the very things that completely destroy us.

A few evenings ago, I was putting up shelves in my garage. I'm kind of obsessed with building them and buying them. I think it's what I'm known for now in my circles—shelves. I'm the shelves guy. "King of Graphs" and "Master of Shelves," these are my identities. But whatever, if you're not utilizing vertical space then you're a sucker.

See? I could take over for Choanna.

Anyways, I had my dog, Walter, in the garage with me. He was on a long leash that was tied to one of my other shelves, and the garage door was open. Walter is the sweetest dog in the world, but he's prone to run after squirrels, birds, and lizards if he sees one. He's also scared the crap out of a few joggers as they've passed by our house. Without thinking, his instincts kick in and he clears the area of all potential pests and murderers. While I was up on my ladder, a neighbor walked by and Walter began to bark and started to run after him, only to be restrained by his leash tied to one of my sturdy shelves. Superior quality woodwork. Real primo stuff.

As I was quieting Walter down, I felt the Holy Spirit speak to me, "That's you, too. You're on a leash." I texted my friend Scott the next day and told him about it. "I think God has kept me restrained from some paths in my life and career I've really wanted but could have been my ruin." Scott said, "That's the protection of God. Every day, I sit with good and godly people who do terrible things. They get what they want and don't know how to handle it."

Our human nature envies what could destroy us and envy itself destroys us. Jealousy is a lie we all must battle, or we will lose to it without even realizing it was defeating us.

♦ ♦ ♦

In Chapter 5 we talked about Peter walking on water. Soon after taking Jesus at his word and stepping out of the boat in faith, Peter denied he had anything to do with Jesus on the night he was arrested. When Jesus was standing on trial, Peter was asked if he was one of his disciples, and he went as far as to say he didn't even know who he was. The third time Peter denied it, Jesus turned and looked right at him. Then, as Jesus had prophesied, a rooster crowed. Peter ran away and wept bitterly,[3] filled with remorse and guilt.

This story breaks my heart every time I read it. It's one of those stories where I hope I'd make the right decision, but if I'm being honest I don't know if I would have. I am weak and fearful. It's why I need a merciful Savior who is strong in my weaknesses.

After his crucifixion and after he had risen from the dead, John 21 describes a scene where Jesus meets up with his disciples who were out fishing one morning. Jesus showed up on the beach, and the moment Peter knew it was him, he got out of the boat again. This time he didn't walk on water. Instead, Peter swam to the shore to be with him.

Jesus asked Peter three times if he loved him, as Peter had denied him three times. When Peter emphatically replied, "Yes, Lord, you know that I love you," Jesus would tell him to feed and take care of "his sheep."[4] Jesus was giving Peter another chance, and even entrusting the future leadership of his church to Peter.

The night Peter denied Jesus, there was another disciple present who often doesn't get mentioned in the retelling of the story. The disciple John went along with Peter that night to follow Jesus' trial. He was actually the one who wrote the book this story was in. He doesn't go into detail about what happened to him while he was there, but we know he was with Jesus throughout the entire progression of the night. He was even at the feet of Jesus when he died on the cross. He was the only disciple to stay with him the whole time.

As Jesus and Peter began to walk along the beach and continue their conversation, John was following behind them. Jesus told Peter he would eventually become a martyr for the Gospel. Quite a big promotion for a guy who wouldn't even admit to being a follower of Jesus. As they walked, Peter looked behind him, saw John, and asked Jesus, "What about him?" Jesus answered, "If I want him to remain alive until I return, what is that to you? You must follow me."[5]

Peter had a quick flare up of JBS. He was comparing himself to someone else and wanting to know what John's story would be. Jesus answered him in the same way I think he answers most of us when we battle JBS: "What about them? You must follow me."

"Jesus, why does someone else have what I want?"

"What about them? You must follow me."

"Jesus, I was on the same track they were on, yet my life looks completely different."

"What about them? You must follow me."

Jesus didn't tell Peter, "Your lives will be different but equal. I've made sure everyone will have the same amount of happiness, sorrow, and vacation days." He simply said, "You must follow me."

Living a life where we ask "What about them?" all the time will drive us to insanity. It's actually a lot like the music video to "Virtual Insanity" by Jamiroquai where the room keeps changing around while the guy is singing. Remember that music video? It was always on VH1's *Pop-Up Video*. Sometimes we're a big shot in a small room. Other times we're a nobody in a big room and the couch keeps moving. In life, the room never stays the same size for too long. You feel confident just long enough for the room to all of a sudden change and expand again when you hit the second verse.

You might feel like you're a celebrity at your company, and then you go to a conference and get around other people in your field who know a lot more than you do. They have more experience, accomplishments, and connections, and it makes you ask yourself, "What the heck am I even doing here? My title is 'Director of Human Affairs.' What does that even mean? It sounds like I'm the leader of adulterers."

Or maybe you're feeling good about yourself as a parent until you go on a field trip and another mom has brought all organic snacks for their child, who is probably named Eartheny. It's like "Anthony," but they're from Oregon. Eartheny's mom says, "Oh, we don't own a TV or an iPad, but Eartheny loves reading his Encyclopedia every night. He is currently learning Spanish, Swahili, and Klingon. Is that your son over there with his shorts on backwards? Aw, your parenting methods are adorable." Boom—Jamiroquai room change. It's virtual insanity.

At any given moment, we're prone to having the room shift on us and make us feel unstable and useless. A repeated story from my life is when another funny guy would show up in my friend circles when I was in school. As we've discussed, I'm not very handsome or smart, cracking jokes was my strength. So when another guy started doing the one thing I thought I could do, it'd completely throw me off, and I would crawl back into my shell. Boom—Jamiroquai room change. The stupid couch moved again.

Peter was being reinstated by Jesus after denying him three times. Jesus was telling him he loved him and had a unique timeline for his life. It was a wonderful, private moment between the two of them. Then Peter looked behind him to see an apostle who had not denied Jesus. Boom— Jamiroquai room change. Peter got insecure.

Yet for all we know, maybe John was jealous of Peter. Peter was the only one who had the faith in Jesus to even get out of the boat and walk on water. What if John thought, "Man, I bet Jesus wished I had the kind of faith and fearlessness Peter has." Boom—Jamiroquai room change.

But these two disciples would eventually fearlessly take the Gospel to the masses, and they would even do it together. They would be a part of many miracles in Jesus' name. They put down their pride, jealousy, and insecurity and moved forward together with a shared purpose. When we keep our eyes on Jesus, we don't need a title or a status to know we matter.

If we're following Jesus, our goal should be to go lower instead of spending our time trying to figure out how to elevate ourselves. In fact, Jesus said, "The greatest among you will be your servant. For those who exalt themselves will be humbled, and those who humble themselves will be exalted."[6]

In the Kingdom of Heaven, there are no big shots. There are only servants.

♦ ♦ ♦

Jealousy is a major roadblock in the church. It can cause quite a bit of turmoil and stunt its growth. Peter and John were integral in launching the early church, and if their JBS had consumed their lives, we likely wouldn't have a big chunk of the New Testament as we know it. The apostles were one in mission, which meant the Gospel spreading anywhere by anyone was good for their mission.

There was another evangelist named Apollos who joined the early church and was preaching the Gospel of Christ as he traveled. The Apostle Paul wrote about him to the church in Corinth, where Apollos had been teaching and leading, but it was a church Paul had planted. Instead of getting jealous of the attention Apollos was receiving from the members, Paul clarified their mission.

When one of you says, "I am a follower of Paul," and another says, "I follow Apollos," aren't you acting just like people of the world? After all, who is Apollos? Who is Paul? We are only God's servants through whom you believed the Good News. Each of us did the work the Lord gave us. I planted the seed in your hearts, and Apollos watered it, but it was God who made it grow. It's not important who does the planting, or who does the watering. What's important is that God makes the seed grow. The one who plants and the one who waters work together with the same purpose.

1 Corinthians 3:4-8

Paul wasn't at war with Apollos; he was grateful for him. He recognized their different roles, but also that they were both equals in serving Jesus. He realized they were both part of something God was already doing. One mission. One body of Christ.

The early church is a great example of how we beat jealousy. They weren't perfect, but they were united.

So how do we beat jealousy? It's really pretty simple. Paul told us to "Rejoice with those who rejoice; mourn with those who mourn. Live in harmony with one another."[7]

The remedy for jealousy is rejoicing.

If you can learn to celebrate with people who are celebrating, you will be invited to a lot more parties. If someone you love has a reason to be glad, you ought to jump in on the party and rejoice with them because that's good for you, too. And wouldn't you want someone to rejoice with you when it's your turn? I remember the night I got engaged. I had planned a party for us to attend right after I surprised Brittany. We showed up to a room full of people we loved, and the joy of our friends celebrating with us made it one of the best nights of my life.

111

I want to be the kind of friend who supports my friends. If my friend is promoting something, I want to share it with people. If my friend is performing or giving a speech, I want to be there. Why not? If I have successful friends then that's good for me, and it means I am good at choosing friends. If my friend is on *The Voice*, you'd better be sure I'm watching and voting for them! If my friend is on *The Bachelorette*, you'd better be sure I'm staging an intervention for them. Life shouldn't be about sticking it to your enemies. It's more fun to rejoice with those who rejoice and to show support in love. You live freer and happier.

Likewise, we must mourn with those who mourn. This is admittedly a hard one because a lot of us don't know how to mourn. Back in the Old Testament days, they would have paid wailers, and not the Bob Marley kind of Wailers. And not the Moby Dick kind of whalers. And not the . . . okay I'll stop. These were professional weepers who were paid to be depressed. (A.K.A. Eeyore's dream job.) They would go through the streets loudly wailing and mourning for whoever was publicly grieving about something. We don't really experience that nowadays, unless you see women leaving a Nicholas Sparks movie. It's hard for us to mourn with those who mourn because we often don't know what to say and fear we'll just make it worse. But if we can learn to "Carry each other's burdens,"[8] we'll see our jealousy fade away as we embrace the hurt of others.

There was an unsolved mystery in my life for a few years that I just discovered the answer to a few months ago. In 2013, I had been suddenly let go from a job in Washington D.C., and I was unsure about the direction my life was going in and what was coming next. I was blogging during that time and trying my best to keep a positive outlook on life. It's hard when your world and daily routine comes to an immediate halt, and the rest of the world keeps moving.

My daily routine changed from getting up, getting dressed, and going to work into waking up, putting on a hoodie, and repeatedly checking the fridge to see if more ice cream had magically appeared. So I would share my struggles and the life lessons I was learning on my blog for whoever wanted to read it, which was probably about eight people.

One day I got an unsigned letter in the mail containing two $50 gift cards to restaurants in D.C. with a note that read, "I know this has been a tough season for you. Hope you can enjoy a few dinner dates with your girlfriend with these cards. God bless you."

I was floored. It was not only nice to have a couple bucks to take my then-girlfriend, Brittany, on a few dates, but it meant so much to me to know I had someone out there who was mourning with me. Someone was in my corner. It was the best kind of support you can give, not just because it was money, but also because it wasn't flippant advice. It was actually stepping into my battle and becoming a part of the story. And also because it was money.

I had no clue who it was from for years until my friend Mark Jones finally spilled the beans and said it was he and his wife, Kirstin, who had sent the gift cards. He told me Kirstin empathized with me and wanted to send some encouragement. I believe her generosity will definitely be rewarded in many ways yet to come, but Mark's reward will now be just a mention in this book. Hope it was worth it, Jones.

Most hurting people don't want your opinion unless they ask for it. But when we step into action, it can go a lot farther than throwing some cliché advice at whoever is in a struggle.

It's hard to be jealous when you're being empathetic. In good times and bad, the more we lay down our opinions and choose to rejoice or weep alongside our friends, we'll begin to see a change not just in the lives of others, but also in our own lives. When I'm happy for my friends, I'm a whole lot happier of a person. Encouragement uplifts the receiver and the giver. It's a win-win option and the best way to fight off our JBS.

> *But God has put the body together, giving greater honor to the parts that lacked it, so that there should be no division in the body, but that its parts should have equal concern for each other. If one part suffers, every part suffers with it; if one part is honored, every part rejoices with it.*
>
> 1 Corinthians 12:24-26

♦♦♦

We discussed in Chapter 2 how insecurity will say, "I'll never have what they have," and our pride tells us, "You deserve it because of how hard you've worked." Jealousy is the best friend of insecurity, and pride is the constant nemesis in our lives.

As I've mentioned earlier, I had a few rough patches in my twenties. I moved from Florida to live with my sister in D.C. in hopes that it was a land of opportunity and jobs as far as the eye can see. A land flowing with milk and honey and 401(k) stock options. But I ended up working on and off as a temp for 10 months while I couldn't even get hired at Best Buy. Many of my days were spent sitting at the kitchen table and applying for jobs for hours to no avail. I also got really good at playing drums on Rock Band, mostly the Lady Gaga songs. Meanwhile, I was still watching my friends get jobs through their connections, and as I'd said, I'd been to about 500 weddings. I was feeling a great mix of pride and insecurity about who I was and my life's decisions, as well as dealing with bitterness toward God, who I felt was holding out on me.

During this period of inconsistency and uncertainty, I was reading through *The Chronicles of Narnia* series by C.S. Lewis, and I was reading *The Horse and His Boy*, which became my favorite in the series. I remember vividly that I was sitting in the kitchen when the boy in the story started taking the words right out of my mouth.

"I do think . . . that I must be the most unfortunate boy that ever lived in the whole world. Everything goes right for everyone except me."[9]

I put the book down for a second and said to myself, "What the heck?" This was hitting me a little too accurately. It was like I had become sucked into the book, like those movies where the kid falls asleep in class and is suddenly living in the story he was learning about.[10]

As the boy in the story was lamenting, Aslan the lion came alongside him and began walking with him. Aslan asked him to tell him why he was so sad. After the boy filled him in, Aslan said, "I do not call you unfortunate," and began to explain how he'd been with him the whole time, even from the moment he was born. Aslan had been behind the scenes making sure the boy got where he needed to be.

The boy began to ask Aslan about why his friend had been wounded on their journey, and Aslan replied, "Child, I am telling you your story, not hers. I tell no one any story but his own." The boy had a similar moment to Peter asking about John, and Aslan's reply was similar to how Jesus replied to Peter.

It's like Aslan was an allegory of Jesus or something. Has anyone ever noticed that?

While I was reading that story, God was speaking to me, encouraging me, and also humbling me by calling out my sin. I was dealing with serious JBS, and I needed to recognize it as my own pride, not just bad luck. When we surrender our lives to God, we can't hold onto our own plans for what we want. It's a daily, hourly, minute-by-minute battle we are always in.

I constantly wrestle with questions like, "What was the point of that?" Like the boy, when things seem to be working against me, I get lost in looking at how things are working for others. But God doesn't have to tell me anyone else's story. He doesn't really even have to tell me my own. He doesn't owe me anything, yet he is working behind the scenes in my timeline. The more I let my pride win, the harder it hurts when my plans conflict with God's plans.

It may seem like we're not getting what we deserve out of life, but fortunately we're not getting what we *truly* deserve. Jesus took the cross for us and took what we actually deserve. He humbled himself more than anyone ever has, and he is now exalted above all other names.

The key to the Kingdom of God is going lower and lower. We're not competing with our brothers and sisters in Christ. If we can learn to humble ourselves, serve, and celebrate, we will do more for the Kingdom of God than many of the big shots we think are doing the most right now.

Chapter 8

Mr. Blue Sky

The Search for Happiness

"People waste their time pondering whether a glass is half empty or half full. Me, I just drink whatever's in the glass."[1]

Sophia, *The Golden Girls*

A few weeks ago, something amazing happened to me: I was happy.

I was using my lunch break to go return a book at the library. For the younger generation, libraries are places we used to visit to read books made out of paper. We had to drive there because Amazon wouldn't drop everything on our doorsteps. Sounds horrible, right? Well, it was. Amazon probably knows more about me than my own mother at this point, and I am fine with it if it means I don't have to go to CVS to buy toothbrushes anymore.

Anyway, things were surprisingly good in that moment. My biggest sale of the year had just closed, people in my family were healthy, and Brittany and I were doing well. The Florida sun was out, and the sky was gorgeous. I was enjoying my drive and singing along with one of my favorite songs, "Mr. Blue Sky" by Electric Light Orchestra, and it just fit the moment so perfectly.

Sun is shinin' in the sky,
There ain't a cloud in sight,
It's stopped rainin',
Everybody's in a play,
And don't you know,
It's a beautiful new day.
Runnin' down the avenue,
See how the sun shines brightly in the city,
On the streets where once was pity,
Mr. Blue Sky is living here today.[2]

I continued my drive, singing along and enjoying the moment while it lasted. When a moment of happiness presents itself, you have to embrace it. Sing loudly in your car. Take your kids to get ice cream. High-five a stranger. Or buy a stranger's five kids ice cream while singing loudly.

I don't want to be a bummer, but I've come to find happiness doesn't willingly stick around too long. I'm not necessarily a Larry David kind of guy who is always looking for reasons to complain about something, but I've realized happiness is a fleeting feeling. So when happiness shows itself, I try and recognize it and hold onto it. Like when my friend Robbie brings chicken nuggets to a house party, that makes me happy.

The lyrics of the song continue on to say, "Mr. Blue, you did it right, but soon comes Mr. Night creepin' over. Now his hand is on your shoulder." I love this song, not just because it's a masterpiece, but because it's an accurate depiction of our lives. Day is followed by night. Happiness is followed by sadness. Like when the chicken nuggets are gone and I'm saddened by how many I ate without taking a breath. Back and forth. Up and down. Happiness is a fleeting moment because Mr. Night is on his way, and he's fighting to take our eyes off of Mr. Blue Sky.

Mr. Blue Sky, please tell us why you had to hide away for so long.

Where did we go wrong?

♦ ♦ ♦

No one tells you adult life is full of so much loneliness.

Well, I guess I just told you. But other than me right now, no one tells you adult life is full of so much loneliness.

Actually, there are a lot of Psalms that talk about being lonely.

Alright, other than me and the Psalms, no one tells you.

Come to think of it, no one tells you about how interest rates on loans work. I wish I'd had a class in high school about that and what terms like "equity" and "escrow" mean. That'd been way more helpful in life than chemistry.

My point is that adult loneliness is not mentioned a whole lot outside of a few songs by Hall & Oates. Growing up, we are constantly surrounded by friends and budding new friendships. We think they are going to be lifelong friends, but most of them turn out to be temporary friendships. They may always be acquaintances thanks to social media, but close friendships are hard to keep and maintain for years and years. It's just how it is. I know. I, too, was shocked to discover that friends aren't necessarily friends forever even if the Lord's the Lord of them.[3]

I had to move a few times in my twenties, and it was tough to start over in a whole new city where many friendships and friend circles had already been formed. It was hard to fit into new groups. Even in my friendships now, whenever they start talking about stories from years before I knew them, it makes me wish I had *my* old friends close by, or even my family.

Making friends as an adult is difficult because you don't have the seemingly endless number of hours you had in your youth to spend with someone. Most friendships revolve around 30-minute lunches and a few hours at a party here and there. We're not doing sleepovers and week-long youth group trips with each other, providing tons of time to connect and bond. Even in the close friendships we make as adults, we often wonder if they really know us. And if they really, truly knew us, would they still like us?

Marriage doesn't even cure loneliness. Admittedly, it does help a lot to know you have someone who is choosing to love you and stand beside you forever. But we cannot put the burden of our perpetual brokenness onto one person. It's not fair for me to expect my wife to fulfill all of my needs. She will never be enough, and I will never be enough for her. Many marriages struggle because husbands and wives have placed false expectations on their spouses, and they expect their partners to give them levels of companionship and encouragement they were never meant to give them or are even capable of giving them.

Back and forth. Up and down. Hills and valleys. We are living in a broken world and fighting the effects of its brokenness every day.

I told you about my "Mr. Blue Sky" morning, but there was another recent morning where I felt completely opposite.

I try and have a morning routine because it helps me feel productive, and it's comforting. I don't have kids yet, so I'm sure this routine will fly out the window the moment we have a baby. Geez, I don't even have kids yet and they're already annoying me. I usually wake up in a fog before my morning coffee, so that's the first thing I grab. Then I try to spend some time reading the Bible and praying, and then I like to do some writing unless there's a house project I have to tackle, or I need to start work early. As the coffee kicks in and I get rolling with the morning, I'm genuinely doing fine.

This particular morning, though, something was off. My routine was the same, but the grogginess of the morning was not wearing off. I had a second cup of coffee, but that didn't help. I started to realize my problem was more than being tired. I had something unsettled inside of me. To put it plainly: I was sad. Mr. Night wasn't letting go of me.

I kissed Brittany goodbye as she left for work and went back into my home office for the day. I began to start my work while still wondering what was going on with me. I can normally compartmentalize stuff, and if I'm upset I will usually know why. Reasons like, *I received bad news about my job*, or, *I'm worried about our finances.* Or even really deep, psychological reasons like: *The Gators lost, or, I ate too many chicken nuggets and now I hate myself.* However, this time I couldn't put my finger on any reason like that, I just felt bummed out.

I was hoping the feeling would go away as I got rolling with my work duties and with some Paul Simon playing. But about 45 minutes into my workday, it still wasn't wearing off. I suddenly had the thought, *When is the last time I cried? Maybe I just need to cry.*

I am not a guy who cries every time I see a sunrise or anything, but I do shed some tears every now and then when certain moments hit me. I'll cry occasionally when I hear moving stories from someone or during a special time with God in worship or prayer, and then, like most people, during painful times in life. It turns out it's healthy to cry. According to the always accurate WebMD, emotional tears contain levels of stress hormones that help relieve our tightened muscles and tension caused by stress.[4] That's probably why you may have seen me crying at the gym. I guess I'm just a health nut.

How was your workout, brah?

Oh bro, I'm feeling so swoll, bro. How about you, bro?

Brah, I just finished legs and back. Total beast mode today. I'm gonna do some cardio and then go cry in the locker room!

You're crushing it, bro!

So I decided I needed to cry. But how? My initial thought was, of course, to go right to the Susan Boyle video. On this morning, however, I needed something that hit a different nerve. I didn't necessarily need to be inspired, I needed to just let it all out. So I took a moment to think of the saddest thing I could, and then I hopped onto YouTube.

I chose the scene from *Dumbo* where Dumbo's mother sings "Baby Mine" to him while he sits outside of her locked cage. As the mother elephant caressed her baby boy with her trunk through the window, she sang these words:

Baby mine, don't you cry.
Baby mine, dry your eyes.
Rest your head close to my heart,
Never to part, baby of mine.[5]

Well, I began to do the exact opposite of what she was telling her son to do. I, a grown man in my thirties, began to cry uncontrollably at my desk watching cartoon elephants. Like, really hard weeping. Shoulders bobbing, tears streaming down my face. I released it like a flood. My dog, Walter, came and sat by my feet because he sensed something was going on and that I might have some serious issues.

I went into the bathroom and began to wash my face only to cry a little bit more into a towel. One benefit of working from home that day was I didn't have to walk by any coworkers after this and lie to them and say, "Oh, I just had a sneeze attack, that's why my eyes are all swollen and red."

Or, "Oh, I was just snorting cocaine in the bathroom. Don't worry." Thankfully, I didn't have to say to anyone, "Yeah, I was balling my eyes out watching Disney movies because I had some repressed feelings of sadness lingering in my soul this morning, and apparently I miss my mom more than I realized. And didn't you know it's healthy to cry, bro? Hey, what's the Jags record this year? Is that a new shirt you're wearing?"

I returned to my desk, and surprisingly felt a whole lot better, like a weight had been lifted off of my shoulders. It was even a little easier to breathe. That evening, I told Brittany about it when she got home from work. I'd hoped she'd come over and hug me and say, "I love having a sensitive man who is in touch with his emotions." Instead, she—the girl of my dreams, my muse—burst out laughing, directly in my face. "What the heck, Jon?" She's my rock. Embarrassed, I laughed and said, "I know, it's the weirdest thing, but crying worked. I felt so much better after it. I might be a genius." She replied, "I'm not sure genius is the right word here."

No one tells you adult life will have moments where you have to cry uncontrollably while watching *Dumbo* clips. We walk through life like a sponge, not even realizing what we're absorbing and how deeply we're holding it in. We gather the dirt of loneliness, depression, self-doubt, insecurity, and anger. Every once in a while, all the dirt we've collected reveals itself whether we want it to or not. Sometimes in really weird ways and spontaneous moments.

"The mouth speaks what the heart is full of."[6] What we've harbored and hoarded inside finds its way out. Even in a loving marriage or surrounded by solid friendships, there is an emptiness we live with inside of us. It's why U2's song "I Still Haven't Found What I'm Looking For"[7] makes more and more sense the older you get.

Being a Christian means we are in the Body of Christ. "We who are many form one body."[8] It means our hope is in Heaven, and we have an eternal purpose and an everlasting promise. It means we are part of a bigger family and a bigger story than we can comprehend.

That said, being a Christian can also lead to a lot of lonely walks home. Christianity doesn't cure loneliness because the very Head of the Body,[9] Christ himself, was often alone. The Gospels say Jesus would withdraw to solitary, lonely places.[10] He grieved and wept.[11] Isaiah prophetically wrote about him, and it wasn't exactly a majestic description.

> *He had no beauty or majesty to attract us to him,*
> *Nothing in his appearance that we should desire him.*
> *He was despised and rejected by mankind,*
> *A man of suffering, and familiar with pain.*
> *Like one from whom people hide their faces,*
> *He was despised, and we held him in low esteem.*
> Isaiah 53:2-3

That isn't the kind of description Jimmy Fallon would say before one of his guests comes out. We can tend to think of Jesus as a stoic, emotionless being floating his way through crowds of people and speaking in a monotone voice, but he was a very real man. We also think, because he was the Son of God, he was unmoved by anything; he used his superpowers to overcome sin and all human emotions. But he was tempted.[12] He was betrayed and then forsaken by friends.[13] He felt pain, abandonment, and loneliness.

On the night of the famous Last Supper, the night before he was crucified, Jesus was praying in the Garden of Gethsemane. Knowing he was heading to the cross, he told his disciples, "My soul is overwhelmed with sorrow to the point of death."[14] As he was praying in anguish, his sweat was like drops of blood falling to the ground.[15] It was the first of many more drops of blood he would lose in the next 24 hours.

"Abba, Father," he said, "Everything is possible for you. Take this cup from me. Yet not what I will, but what you will."

Mark 14:36

When the men came to arrest him, "all the disciples deserted him and fled."[16] He was on his own to face the crowds and false accusations that would be thrown at him. He was on his way to die for our sins.

The older I get, the more I love this story. Maybe that sounds odd to say, but I don't love it because it's an enjoyable story to curl up with in bed. I have come to love it because it is the most human we ever see Jesus. The images I have of a stoic God-man fall away when I read it. Here, Jesus felt the weight of the world's sin on his shoulders, and he was broken down by it. He fully knew what he had to do and what he had to endure, and he fully knew his perfect sacrifice was about to shift the cosmos, and he pleaded with the Father to find another way to redeem the world. But he didn't have his request granted. The Father said, "No."

A few years ago, I was also grieving in prayer. I wasn't about to die for the sins of the world, and I surely wasn't a perfect man, but I was overwhelmed. As I've mentioned earlier, I was once unemployed and living at my sister's house, wrestling with loneliness and lack of purpose in my life. I'd tried everything I knew to do since I'd graduated from college, and three years later I still had no direction. I wasn't sitting around on the couch all day not trying. I was putting myself out there in every way I knew how, and nothing was clicking. I was frustrated, angry, and sad.

On this day I was praying alone in the house and kneeling by the side of my bed. "God, I hate this. I hate all of this. Sometimes I wish I was an atheist because then I wouldn't have to know there is a God in Heaven who is seeing me like this but doing nothing about it. Why isn't anything working? Why am I unable to see any progress? Why am I still so alone?" It felt like I was right back in my car, driving through Gainesville after being turned away by the prison all over again. I thought absolutely nothing in my life had progressed since that moment in the car. I'd lost my time and energy, yet had gained nothing.

I assume you've had similar thoughts, too. Where is the God of miracles I've heard so much about? The God with infinite power who says he loves me, where is he at? What is he waiting for?

When I had stopped talking, I put my face down on my bed, exhausted and motionless. Even though I had asked God so many "why" questions, I didn't really expect any answers, and I didn't really know if I even wanted one. But in the silence of the moment, I felt the still, small voice of God speak to my heart, "I'm making you like my Son."

That was all I heard, but I understood the message. God wasn't beating me up, but he was letting me endure loneliness and brokenness because Jesus had been lonely and broken. He was letting my strength and abilities fail me because Jesus gave up his own strength. He was letting my pride die because Jesus was humble.

When we are lonely, we are more like Jesus. When we are abandoned, we are more like Jesus. When we are hurting, we are more like Jesus. But we are never forsaken because Jesus was already forsaken for us.

Pain is not a punishment, it is part of the process of life. I wish I could say it wasn't. I have never liked the phrase, "I'm too blessed to be stressed." I think I understand its sentiment, "I have a higher hope than the troubles of the world," but it's just not a truthful statement. At some point, our pain can hit a breaking point where no amount of blessing can turn a frown upside down.

"Did you know you use way more muscles to frown than to smile? C'mon, big guy!"

"Do you know how many muscles I'm using to restrain myself from throat punching you right now?"

When I'm hurting, I need the truth spoken over me, but I don't need a random Bible verse flippantly thrown in my face. When someone is visiting their loved one in a hospital, you'd be an idiot to walk up to them in the waiting room and say, "Count it all joy, my brother. This produces perseverance." Is it a true statement? Sure. But being a Christian doesn't mean we always have to snap out of honest emotions and feelings. So instead of saying, "I'm too blessed to be stressed," you could just start saying, "I'm too blessed to be stressed if I can just ignore how horribly depressed I actually am!"

I don't believe we're meant to live with a defeated, depressed attitude forever, but we will always be fighting off the struggles of the earth. Still, in all of our trials, we can know they have a purpose, and we can know we, too, have a purpose in the midst of trials. That's the hope of our faith in Jesus.

Let us fix our eyes on Jesus, the author and perfecter of our faith, who for the joy set before him endured the cross, scorning its shame, and sat down at the right hand of the throne of God. Consider him who endured such opposition from sinners, so that you will not grow weary and lose heart.

Hebrews 12:1-3

As Jesus lowered himself into our world and onto our level, as he took on loneliness, and as he endured the suffering of the cross, he did it for the joy set before him. It's crazy to think there could be any element of joy in the ugliness of a crucifixion, yet that is the difference between happiness and joy. Happiness has to present itself, whereas joy will hide itself in the midst of suffering and pain. True joy weaves itself into all areas of our lives, whether good or bad, because joy is a fruit of the Spirit. If you've committed your life to the Lord, you've probably experienced the effects of true joy without realizing it.

We talked in Chapter 4 about how following Christ doesn't automatically make us "happy all the day." So joy doesn't always mean we're smiling, but it means we have a hope that can't be shaken by anything in this world. Psalm 94:19 says, "When anxiety was great within me, your consolation brought me joy." The Psalmist didn't say, "I'm too blessed to be anxious," they said, "I am feeling the effects of a broken world, yet I have a greater hope." Paul repeatedly wrote about his great joy while he was in prison because the presence of Jesus was with him in spite of his circumstances.

We will all experience sadness and loneliness, but we don't have to experience hopelessness. There is more at work than we can see, and there is an eternal purpose to momentary struggles.

Therefore we do not lose heart. Though outwardly we are wasting away, yet inwardly we are being renewed day by day. For our light and momentary troubles are achieving for us an eternal glory that far outweighs them all. So we fix our eyes not on what is seen, but on what is unseen, since what is seen is temporary, but what is unseen is eternal.

2 Corinthians 4:16-18

♦ ♦ ♦

When we bought our home in Jacksonville, the roof was in horrible condition. It hadn't been replaced in over 17 years, and in Florida, that is an eternity for roofs, as they have to endure significant heat and torrential rainfalls. We knew it was ugly, but it wasn't at the top of our to-do list because my wife has a high tolerance for unattractive things, and let me just beat everyone to the joke: That's how she was able to marry me.

Did you have a good laugh at my expense? You feel good about yourself? Alright, let's move on.

We lived under that ugly roof for many months. At least twice a week we'd have a roofing company stop by and knock on our door, causing my dog Walter to bark uncontrollably, and then they would proceed to ask me if I knew my roof was in bad shape. I'd answer them while holding Walter back from running out the front door to scare away the potential murderers, "Yes, we are planning on getting the roof fixed, we just don't have the money right now. My friend David is a roofer, and he's going to handle it when the time comes. Thanks." They would continue with their sales pitch about how they could help. One time after I'd gone through my usual spiel, a salesman had the audacity to say, "Yeah, your neighbor said you wouldn't get it fixed." To which I replied, "Well, he's a nosy idiot." You know me, just spreading the love of Christ. Unsurprisingly, we haven't exactly been invited over for drinks since then.

That is how sadness works. Sadness is a door-to-door salesman barging in on your day. It doesn't care if you have a "Do not solicit" sign on the edge of your neighborhood, it ignores all of your plans and makes you deal with it. You can try to ignore it, but it will just keep coming and your dog will keep barking until you finally answer the door.

Happiness doesn't work that way. Happiness is that person you know who you secretly have a friend-crush on because you think they are just the coolest, yet they never come to any of your parties. No matter how many times you invite them over, they forget or have other plans. And they never, ever hit "Confirm" on a Facebook invite. But every now and then, you end up hanging out with them and it's just as glorious as you'd imagined it would be.

That's happiness.

Happiness will occasionally present itself, but we usually have to hunt down the good if we want to experience it. Some people are so stressed out, I don't know how they survive without spontaneously combusting. People who are always on edge like this are not hunting down the good; they are just answering the door for whatever shows up. Most knocks on the door aren't good things, so they are always upset. They are miserable to be around, and it's probably miserable to be them. In a letter to his brother, C.S. Lewis said, "I begin to suspect that the world is divided not only into the happy and unhappy, but into those who like happiness and those who, odd as it seems, really don't."[17]

The "Mr. Blue Sky" lyrics go on to say more about the struggle between Mr. Blue Sky and Mr. Night:

Mr. Blue, you did it right,
But soon comes Mr. Night creepin' over,
Now his hand is on your shoulder,
Never mind, I'll remember you this way.

I love how that verse ends with choosing to remember Mr. Blue Sky, even when he's been hiding away. Happiness is often a choice we make. We choose what we dwell on, and what we magnify will change how we act. Are we magnifying our daily grievances as we're fighting our battles, or are we lifting up the One who has already won every battle we'll ever fight?

The Bible is full of verses telling us to magnify the Lord because it's our only shot at hope. The Psalms are flooded with calls to praise the Lord. David even commanded his soul to bless the Lord,[18] whether his soul wanted to or not. It's just like when your wife makes you go to HomeGoods with her on a Saturday. Worship has very little to do with waiting for your church band to play the right Passion song that makes you happy. Worship is a spiritual war. We're fighting to magnify Jesus while so many other cares of our lives are knocking on our doors and trying to magnify themselves.

We hunt for happiness by living with gratefulness. Counting our blessings instead of being angry about what we don't have. If this sounds simplistic, it's because it absolutely is. God doesn't call us to always be happy, but he does call us to worship. And as we worship the Most High, we will see the darkness fade away. The joyful blue skies may be hidden at times, but they are out there. Don't let the night tell you otherwise.

In him was life, and that life was the light of all mankind. The light shines in the darkness, and the darkness has not overcome it.

John 1: 4-5

Chapter 9

The Hopes and Fears
of all the Years

Getting Past the Past

Nick: "Don't let your past dictate who you are, but let it be part of who you will become."
Toula: "Nick, that's beautiful."
Nick: "Yeah, that Dear Abby really knows what she's talking about."[1]

My Big Fat Greek Wedding

One night in college some of my friends were having dinner at a restaurant late in the evening. College is a wonderful period of life where you can make horrible food choices at any time of the day but still not have to worry about signing up for Weight Watchers. Someone had ordered a giant chocolate dessert for the group to split. As it showed up at the table, my friend Brandon joyously proclaimed, "Oh man, we are going to have some nightmares tonight, guys!"

There was a pause of silence at the table, and then someone said, "What are you talking about?" Brandon explained, "You know, because if you eat chocolate at night you . . . have nightmares." As the words were coming out of his mouth, he began to realize it was just something his mom had told him as a kid to keep him from eating chocolate at night. Yet, he'd never verbalized it and analyzed it as an adult. In spite of the warning, I heard the dessert was eaten and they all slept soundly without any nightmares.

I find this story hilarious for obvious reasons, but I also like it because I can relate to it. We all have certain beliefs, practices, phrases, or habits we've held onto from our upbringings that, when verbalized to others as adults, we find out are not common, or worse—nowhere near normal.

For example, one day Brittany and I were eating popcorn and I was drinking Coke out of a glass, but I was dipping my popcorn into the Coke and then eating it. She gave me a puzzled look and asked why I was doing that. I had never realized how weird it was until that very moment. I remembered it was because I saw my sister Melissa doing it all the time growing up, which is why I started doing it. Why she started doing it, I still don't know. She's just a creative genius, I guess. A true visionary.

I'm sure your family has interesting quirks or practices you've had delayed revelations about, too. It's not always weird stuff like my sister's Coke Fondue idea. We hold onto political ideologies and religious beliefs. I remember in elementary school, all of us Christian kids were disgusted to have a Presidential Physical Fitness Award signed by Bill Clinton. I had a 9-year-old friend throw his in the trash. We were godly little Republicans, you know. We didn't know anything about politics. We'd only heard our parents talk negatively about him, and that was enough for us.

Our past affects our present. The impressions we receive as children and the choices we make in life, along with their resulting consequences, stick with us for ages. Experiences from our past take up residence with the hibernating bear and burrow deep inside of the caves of our minds.

◆ ◆ ◆

When discussing the events of our lives and the decisions we've made along the way, people often say something to the effect of, "It doesn't matter now, what's done is done." There is truth in that sentiment. We are not necessarily who we were in our pasts, and we shouldn't allow our mistakes to haunt us. But to say our pasts don't matter would be inaccurate, maybe even a little delusional. Our pasts do matter.

If our pasts never mattered, then we would have no hope for our futures, because our futures and the moments currently unfolding will soon become our pasts. If nothing in our pasts matter, then by that logic it would mean nothing yet to come would matter either. It also really ruins the plot of *Back to the Future*.

Unfortunately, the past can be difficult to deal with, which is why we like to say it doesn't matter. It's easier to pick out the pieces of our pasts that we enjoyed and say those are the only moments that matter. That's like going through Lucky Charms and only eating the marshmallows. It may be more appealing, but it's not healthy. And the next person to reach for the cereal box is going to pour themselves a marshmallow-less bowl of sadness. You and I are the results of our pasts, both the good and the bad parts. We can't just move past the past because we are always carrying it with us.

There's an ancient proverb that says, "You take the good, you take the bad, you take them both, and there you have the facts of life."[2] Powerful stuff. It's true, life is full of highs and lows. We all have awkward interactions, exhilarating victories, and disappointing conversations. Each experience we go through works to develop our character. Billions of moments come together to shape who we are, like a giant mosaic piece of artwork. The good moments give us something to hope for, so we're more likely to highlight those instances. But we can't always shake off the bad moments like they don't matter, no matter what Taylor Swift tells you.

I've shared about my chandelier meltdown and about how I have been uptight about taking care of my possessions. Recently, the hibernating bear came out and gave me a reason for why I'm like that.

I didn't grow up with a ton of money, so if a toy broke, well, that was usually it for me and that toy. I distinctly remember one instance from when I was very young where a kid in my neighborhood broke my plastic pirate sword I'd just gotten in St. Augustine, FL. I showed the broken sword to my mom and asked if I could get a new one, and she said no. St. Augustine was over two hours away so it made sense why we couldn't replace it, but I still remember thinking, "My sword is gone forever." So I never let that kid play with my toys again, and I started keeping a tight hold on my possessions. As a result of all of my toys being valuable to me, I now take really good care of my things, and I get mad when others don't care for them the way I do, either with my things or their own possessions. I've never understood what it's like to leave your video game controller next to an open box of pizza, or how anyone could flippantly throw their laptop charger into their backpack without wrapping it up properly. It's so reckless! Evidently, the events of my past have continual effects on who I am and how I behave today. I'm still that kid who is nervous of losing it all and never getting it back.

I'm sure the hibernating bear will continue to reveal to me all of the other ticks and habits I've yet to discover resulting from events in my life. Our pasts clearly affect how we behave now. If it's in the past, it matters, and it is definitely influencing our present.

♦ ♦ ♦

Beyond the suppressed inclinations the hibernating bear exposes to us over time, we are also living with the effects of more prominent experiences from our pasts. Whether they're the choices we made or moments we had no control over, we can't just ignore them. Most of us live with regrets and the sting of memories we wish we could change. While we can't do much about many of the experiences we've faced, we are given a choice in how we respond and how we move forward.

When Brittany and I first started dating, she was still dealing with the fallout of relationships in college where she had been cheated on and treated horribly. It was hard for her to trust me, even though I'd never given her a reason not to. But for me, after having been single for years and only dating on and off, I had grown accustomed to things not working out. So I didn't care to work too hard at a romantic relationship. As a result, we had a rocky start. At any sign of conflict, she'd view me as a threat and push me away, yet always hoping I would fight for us. However, I'd just say, "Alright, cool. I'm out."

One night in particular, we were supposed to go to a dinner theater show in Old Town Alexandria. During an argument on the phone earlier that day, she said she didn't want to talk to me for the whole weekend. It was a game of Chicken, and she thought I'd try to work things out. True to my passive, apathetic dating style, I just took my roommate Mike instead. To Mike's credit, he was quite a gentleman and we had a nice date together, but he never called me again. Typical men. For Brittany and me, the events of our past dating experiences were driving our present decisions.

That's the danger of living with regret. Past regrets are also future fears that stunt our progress and growth. We're afraid it'll happen like it did before and we'll be hurt or hurt someone else. A big reason I was single for so long was because I was afraid of feeling pain or inflicting the kind of pain I'd felt in break ups onto someone else. Also, I'm not exactly Ryan Gosling, and I didn't have a lot of girls chasing me down. But, I mean, mostly the pain thing was probably the main reason. Brittany and I finally found peace in our relationship when we said, "We're in this. No more games of Chicken. We're not going to flippantly break up anymore. Love doesn't quit like that." The commitment to acknowledge we were not copies of the people we'd dated in our pasts released us into a brand new future we could move forward into and build on together. No more Chicken dating.

Note to self: Pitch "Chicken Dating" show to the VH1. The person who stays in the dysfunctional relationship the longest wins $100,000. Or even like actual chickens dating each other in a coop. Both ideas are on par with their standards of programming.

When we live with regret and future fears, we live with a defense system around us. We build walls to make sure we're not hurt again, and while it may be effective in avoiding pain, we are not living as God made us to live. We can't truly love or allow ourselves to be loved without being vulnerable. We can't give ourselves away if we're keeping an escape route in our pocket. Intimate love requires letting others into the places where they could hurt us the most. I'm not going to pretend that it isn't scary or risky. It's terrifying.

There is a popular recurring nightmare many people have about suddenly being naked in public. I actually had that dream the other night. Luckily, it's only ever been a dream for me. (I think?) I started wondering why this is such a common dream, and why the thought of being naked in public is so mortifying and embarrassing. I think one of the reasons it unnerves us is because when we are naked we are completely exposed, and there is no way to hide any of our flaws, or what we perceive are our flaws. We assume we're being judged. It's terrifying to let our walls down, especially our walls of clothing. That's why so many one-night stands require so much alcohol.

Sex has been misused for centuries as a way for people to selfishly experience pleasure. Sex was created by God to specifically reflect our relationship with him. We're completely bare in his presence. We can't hide our flaws. We're totally vulnerable, and there are no walls between us. It's an intimacy we're not meant to share with random strangers or be forced into under the manipulation of someone else. Sex takes us back to the Garden of Eden. Genesis 2:25 says Adam and Eve were "naked and felt no shame." There was no embarrassment or façade. Marital sex is the joining of two imperfect beings into a holy union. Likewise, with God, we are joined to him by removing all we think we can hide. He sees us as perfect and holy through the lens of the blood of Christ.

Only when we experience the perfect love of God can we begin to tear our walls down and truly give love. "There is no fear in love. But perfect love drives out fear."[3] God sees all the flaws we try to hide and loves us just the same. Our past decisions and circumstances have no bearing on the love God has for us. We can be vulnerable and without fear.

Some of us have spent years and years collecting shame and insecurity without even realizing it. Our pasts hold us back from embracing the love of God and the love of others. But through God's love and grace, we can be completely exposed and feel no shame.

You are who you are because of your past, but you are not your past.

You are a product of your past, but you are not defined by it.

There are a few superhero movies I really wanted to enjoy. I've watched them a few times and tried to appreciate them, but I just can't. The first is *Spider-man 3* and the second is *Batman v Superman: Dawn of Justice.* I don't consider myself knowledgeable enough in nerd culture to speak out on much in the comic book universe, but I do have some strong opinions about these movies.

Both movies suffer from the same issue with their plots: too many villains. In *Spider-man 3*, Spider-man is fighting the Sandman, the Symbiote, the Green Goblin, and Venom, and he is also dealing with girl problems and issues with his boss. In *Batman v Superman*, they are battling each other, random bad guys, one of the biggest villains ever, and whatever the heck Lex Luthor is up to for no defined reason whatsoever. Every time Lex was on screen I wanted to slap myself in the face. Was he just angry because he's crazy? Crazy because he's angry? What was his goal? They thought if they had him talk fast enough then they wouldn't really have to define why he's . . . I'm sorry. I'm getting off track.

If you go back and watch these movies (which I am not recommending) you'll notice each story piled on way too many villains, leaving the audience clueless as to what the hero's motivation was and why any of it actually mattered beyond the idea of them thinking, "These guys are bad guys and I need to stop them because I'm a superhero and that's what I do." I may own multiple Pauly Shore movies on DVD, but even I know that's bad writing. In great story writing, you feel the tension of the conflict and get drawn into the struggle of the hero overcoming internal doubts, which brings a greater meaning to battling the external foes. In these two movies, the writers and producers just figured if they threw enough bad guys, fights, and explosions into the mix then most people wouldn't care about the plot. Unfortunately, they were right and both movies were commercial successes.

Most of us haven't written plots for movies with $250 million budgets, but we do a lot of the writing of our own stories. And while we can recognize the error of too many villains in movies, we don't recognize it as easily in our lives.

Some villains are easy to spot, like a mean boss, a nitpicking mother-in-law, a bully of an older brother, or Karen in the church choir who gives you passive aggressive singing tips even though she can't stay on pitch to save her life. *You're not the choir director, Karen! You shouldn't even have a solo, and everyone knows it.* These kinds of villains are easy to spot because they are actively and obviously working against us. Some villains are harder to notice because they are internal, and we are the ones writing them into our stories. Maybe they're the weird habits and ticks we've picked up over the years from our families or through our experiences, or maybe it's the villain of jealousy we talked about in Chapter 7. We already have so many other villains to fight in our day-to-day lives, why should we add our regrets into the mix as well? Why waste the energy on hating and battling ourselves?

Because of our past experiences and future fears, many of us exhaust ourselves every day fighting internal battles. Our growth is stunted because we can't forgive ourselves. If we can't forgive ourselves, it is extremely hard to accept the forgiveness God gives. If we're unable to forgive ourselves, it's a sign we haven't fully accepted the grace God is freely giving.

Grace can be hard for us to understand because we're so used to living in a world where people are punished. It feels good to see murderers thrown in prison. It feels good to watch terrorist regimes be brought down. It even gives us a boost of pride to watch a corrupt coworker get fired. We live in a very cause-and-effect world. As a result, the idea of grace wiping away all our punishment can be a hard concept to truly believe and receive.

I've often heard God's grace described as "scandalous." Nowadays, we mostly identify scandals with Washington, or Kerry Washington, and we don't connect it with amazing grace. Yet, God's grace is absolutely scandalous. One definition of scandalous is "causing general public outrage by a perceived offense against morality or law." Boom. A cause-and-effect world demands punishment for our crimes, which is why God's supernatural grace is an offense against our concept of morality and the laws of our society.

Mercy is the relinquishing of punishment. Grace is stepping into the place of the one who is to be punished. Grace becomes the villain in place of the villainous.

But where sin increased, grace increased all the more, so that, just as sin reigned in death, so also grace might reign through righteousness to bring eternal life through Jesus Christ our Lord.

Romans 5:20

When a sinless Savior willingly got up on a cross, he created the greatest scandal of all time. He became the villain. "God made him who had no sin to be sin for us, so that in him we might become the righteousness of God."[4] He stood in our place and took the punishment we were destined for so that 2,000 years later we wouldn't be fighting ourselves. He took the curse so we would have the gift of freedom and abundant life.

Either the sacrifice of Christ was fully effective for us or it was completely worthless. There is no option in between where the cross was slightly powerful enough to take the punishment for some of your sins but not for the rest. Jesus paid it all. Everything. The cross was enough. Stop trying to pay for your sins by holding onto guilt, fear, and shame. Stop putting yourself on a cross when Jesus took the cross once and for all.

You are not defined by your past. You are defined by who God says you are. You are defined by the scandalous grace of Jesus. You can be "naked and without shame."

◆ ◆ ◆

Also, in Genesis, we're told of a boy named Joseph who was destined for greatness. Yet before he was made second-in-command of all of Egypt, he was thrown into a pit by his brothers, then sold into slavery, and then tossed into prison and forgotten. From the time Joseph was 17 years old until he was 30, he was living out a continual nightmare. Just when it would seem like things were finally changing for him, he'd get knocked back down. However, the Bible repeatedly says, "The Lord was with Joseph"[5] throughout all of it.

In Genesis 41, Joseph, the man who was once a slave and prisoner, was placed in command over all of Egypt, second only to Pharaoh. He literally went from rags to riches. It's easy to look at Chapter 41 and say that the Lord was with Joseph. By then, he'd become a big shot who had been given power and wealth. The Lord surely was with him and promoted him. But if we say the Lord was with Joseph in Chapter 41, then we have to say the Lord was with him in Chapter 37 when he was thrown into a pit and sold as a slave, and we have to say the Lord was with him in Chapter 39 when he was still a slave and falsely accused of rape and thrown into prison, and we have to say the Lord was with him in Chapter 40 when he was stuck in prison for years.

Joseph was being shaped throughout all of his trials, and by the trials themselves. It wasn't easy or quick. As we know, it takes a lot to get 'em right when you're learning the facts of life. The crappy, painful, depressing facts of life. His honor and character were being developed throughout each ordeal, and they provided him valuable lessons, equipping him to be the leader he needed to be.

We all want to be Chapter 41 Joseph. We want to be standing on top victorious, but we wouldn't have had the Joseph of Chapter 41 without the Joseph of Chapters 37-40. As Joseph took charge of Egypt, he was not defined as the defenseless boy thrown into a pit by his own brothers. He was not defined as a slave or a prisoner.

Joseph's past didn't define him at all. His past shaped him and prepared him.

Joseph's story is not memorable and inspiring because he was born into power. It's inspiring because he lived a life filled with real struggles. Who wants to watch a movie that begins with Luke Skywalker blowing up the Death Star and getting awarded? Who wants to watch Rudy score a winning touchdown in the first five minutes? Or who wants to see Pauly Shore's new father-in-law love him the first time they meet? Good stories all have character development because of the challenges and trials they face.

What you've been through is not just about you, it's about others. If you have a messed up past, but you're reading this right now, then you also have a testimony. Jesus is so good he can turn our failures into his glory.

Revelation 12:11 talks about the power to overcome by the blood of the Lamb and the word of our testimonies. We have the power to overcome our fears and regrets through the blood of the Lamb, which is what Jesus has already done on the cross, and the word of our testimony, which is what Jesus is doing in and through us.

Through the power of the Holy Spirit, we can hold to the truth that God is using our experiences for our good, just as he did with Joseph. Instead of just erasing our bad memories, he is gathering our pain and producing something good and for his glory—our testimonies.

Our testimonies are meant to be shared with others. So many of us are scared to reveal too much because we fear the judgment of others. While it's true a few people may judge you, many more people need to know what God has done in you and for you. We need to hear the word of your testimony. Your story is powerful because it's honest. It's real life. And through the power of the blood of the Lamb, we don't have to be ashamed. You are not a prisoner of your past, you are no longer the villain, and you are not your failure.

We are not defined by our pasts, and we're not defined by our futures. If it was up to us getting things right, we'd never do enough. If it were up to us being good, we'd never be good enough. We'll never be smart enough or brave enough. The scandalous grace of God says we are enough because he loves us. That's it.

We are enough because we are enough. Jesus loves us because he loves us.

Anyone who belongs to Christ has become a new person. The old life is gone; a new life has begun.

2 Corinthians 5:17 (NLT)

♦ ♦ ♦

As I write this chapter, Christmas is just a few weeks away. Yesterday I heard a middle school marching band horn section playing outside of a grocery store trying to earn a few bucks for their program. If you've never heard a middle school marching band horn section play, it sounds like ducks dying a slow, painful death. If you've never heard the sound of ducks dying a slow painful death, it sounds like Chandler's girlfriend Janice from *Friends* laughing at her own joke, while she is dying a slow, painful death. So yeah, the band wasn't exactly going to be touring with Springsteen any time soon.

As I walked by, I managed to make out that they were playing "O Little Town of Bethlehem," and it's a song I actually hadn't heard this Christmas season yet. As I sang the lyrics in my head, I realized they would be the best way to end this chapter.

> *O little town of Bethlehem,*
> *How still we see thee lie,*
> *Above thy deep and dreamless sleep,*
> *The silent stars go by.*
> *Yet in thy dark streets shineth the everlasting Light,*
> *The hopes and fears of all the years*
> *are met in Thee tonight.*[6]

Chapter 10

Faithfully Unfaithful

I Will Back Down (Sorry, Tom Petty)

"I'm a great quitter. It's one of the few things I do well. I come from a long line of quitters. My father was a quitter, my grandfather was a quitter. I was raised to give up."[1]

George Costanza, *Seinfeld*

Recently, I was having lunch with my friend Sam, who is also in his thirties, and we were discussing how getting older has its benefits because we care less and less about what people think of us. I now wear sweatpants in public without shame; I'm actually kind of proud of it. My wife was appalled the first time I wore sweatpants to the movies, and now she is all about it because she realizes how wise I am. As you age, you become either more confident or more apathetic, or maybe it's a little bit of both.

Our mindsets change as we progress through time. Scientific studies have shown that our brains physically change.[2] You start saying stuff like, "We really need this rain," "That's not worth the calories," and, "I'm glad those plans fell through because I didn't want to go anyway." When you're in your teens and twenties, being flaky and unorganized can be seen as endearing, and people will say, "Oh, he's a free spirit." When 30 hits, they start saying, "He's not marriage material."

That's why I find myself living off of my calendar more and more. It's not that life necessarily gets busier, but our activities carry more weight. My time seems to move faster and is now more valuable to me because of the role I have as a husband and a full-time employee. I have to stay on schedule.

Here's what getting lunch with a friend looks like in college:

"Hey, my class got canceled. Want to grab lunch?"
"Sure!"

Now here's what it looks like in your thirties:

"Hey, would you like to get lunch?"
"Yes, let's see . . . I'm free three weeks from Thursday. Oh, and I can't eat bread anymore."

I miss the freewheeling days of my youth when I believed anything was possible. I miss having big dreams and faith in God to do the impossible. There were no limits. People could change, and the world could be changed. All it would take was a little can-do attitude and the faith of a mustard seed.

Now I struggle with the increasing weight of my decisions. I'm less inclined to throw caution to the wind and risk everything, because as I get older I feel like I have more to lose. If you're a football coach and you risk a two-point conversion to win the game, you're a hero if it works. But if your quarterback gets sacked, you're an idiot, and it's time to get fired. When you take a risk and the outcome is positive, it's great, but there are many times a risk is taken and it doesn't pan out. It's not romantic to sleep on floors and pursue your dreams of being a musician if you have a family who needs food, shelter, and Netflix. It can be hard to be a wide-eyed dreamer when you're worried about keeping your job.

Our responsibilities increase. The hibernating bear tells you, "You'd better play it safe. Make wise investments of your time, energy, and money. And have you watched *The Crown* yet? That's some good television." The older we get, the harder the risks hurt when they don't work out in our favor. So we stop taking risks and pursue comfort. The lines between wisdom and fear begin to blur.

If I restrain myself from moving forward with a certain decision, is that wise or am I being fearful and lacking faith? Is it wise to save my money, or should I be giving more away? Should we move to a new city because I feel a bit unsatisfied and restless, or is it my selfish ambitions just tempting me at getting more for myself? There are countless questions we wrestle through as we gain more responsibilities and have more to lose.

One struggle in my walk with God is knowing I'm supposed to dream big, but I've dreamed big and failed, so it makes me want to stop dreaming altogether. I've prayed prayers of faith, stepped out in faith, and then found out life isn't one big prosperity sermon; sometimes all the faith in the world doesn't seem to move even the smallest of obstacles in our way. So if something's not working and we're not seeing immediate results, it makes it hard to keep following through. It's easier to cut your losses and move on.

Do you feel that same tension? Do you wonder if you're kidding yourself in attempting some endeavor, or is it something you quit? Is it wisdom or fear? Wisdom is of God, fear isn't. But how do we ever know which is which?

All the confusion can lead us away from being full of hope and instead move us toward drowning in cynicism. You lose faith in yourself and in others as the world chips away at you. In the information age, trending topics and angry opinions fly at us from everywhere. It's like being in the middle of a dodgeball match. Everyone's an expert on every subject when we have the internet at our fingertips. So we have to defend ourselves, and that's when cynicism steps in. Cynicism protects our egos and keeps us from putting any skin in the game because we can just sit on the sidelines making cranky comments. We lose the optimistic, youthful hope we had when we let cynicism take over.

After some time, cynicism becomes exhausting. It's so tiring always being angry and on your guard and ready to debate anyone who would challenge your thinking. Cynicism doesn't let you rest; it only leads you to burn out. You can't always be in an adrenaline-fueled fight mode. I'm looking at you again, CrossFitters.

So then cynicism crushes us into apathy as we get caught up in the demands of our everyday lives. Our passions don't put food on the table; real work does. So we let our dreams die. As the dreams of our youth fade into the background of our lives, many of us lose sight of any goals altogether. We get stuck in our day-to-day lives just trying hard enough to meet the demands of our families and jobs. It's exhausting to have goals outside of what a day already requires of us, especially when dreams so very seldomly come true. It's all too tiring, so it's easier to be apathetic.

It happens the same way in our spiritual lives. Sure, we love the Lord and go to church, but we struggle to believe life can bring anything more than momentary bursts of happiness. At one point we may have chased God with wide-eyed faith, believing the Almighty could do the impossible, but time causes our faith to evolve into merely a quiet relationship with him. We follow God out of a sense of duty but lose the passion. "If I show up to church and put some money in the plate, that's good enough, right?" We are standing face to face with the God of miracles, but we start to view him in the same way we view our boss at work.

This is all part of a cycle I've noticed in my own life. We evolve through stages. Hope transitions into cynicism which moves us to apathy. Then, after I'm apathetic for too long, I get restless sitting in that stage. The restlessness leads me back to hope. I get a burst of energy and want to try something new. So I put on "Man in the Mirror" by Michael Jackson and get to work on making a change. Maybe it's moving to a new city or a new job. Then, after some time, the process inevitably repeats itself again because you realize your problems are surprisingly similar wherever you go.

I call this perpetual process the Cycle of Crap.

Hope → Cynicism → Apathy → Restlessness → Repeat

Apathy and cynicism rob us of the awe and wonder that could be filling our lives. There are moments when I feel like anything is possible, but then real life brings me back down to reality. I have to be responsible. Can you mix a life full of wonder with a life that pays the bills? Can we really live our entire lives with passion and faithfulness to God in a world that throws doubt in our faces every day?

Is there a way to break this cycle? I want more to life than just the daily grind. I want to know my life is made up of more than waking, working, and sleeping, but it feels unrealistic to have the faith of a child when we have to be adults.

Yet Jesus said, "Unless you change and become like little children, you will never enter the kingdom of heaven."[3] So then it must be possible to live with wonder and responsibility at the same time. No matter how far we feel from our dreams or how unrealistic it might seem that anything new could begin in our lives, it is always possible with God. After all, we're talking about a God who does new things all the time.

"Forget the former things;
do not dwell on the past.
See, I am doing a new thing!
Now it springs up; do you not perceive it?
I am making a way in the wilderness
and streams in the wasteland."

Isaiah 43:18-19

We give up too quickly. Even writing this very chapter has made me want to quit this book. Sometimes we stand too close to our lives or projects to see any flaws, and sometimes we're standing too close to one major flaw and it's all we can see. We have to step back and try to see it from God's view. God isn't cynical or apathetic. When we look at our lives we often see a concrete jungle, yet through Christ, we should see a massive, fertile ground where anything can grow. I don't care how bleak your life feels, God can always grow something new. To quote *Jurassic Park* one last time in this book, "Life finds a way."

♦ ♦ ♦

My mom's mom, Bernadine Evearitt, died when I was only 12, but I am so thankful I got to be a part of her incredible life. She was hilarious and loving and also a saint. She would pray for, write to, and encourage missionaries all over the world long before the Internet. I'm talking hand-written letters here. Can you imagine living like that in the primitive dark ages of 1992? Yikes.

She was also known all over town as an amazing storyteller. She'd go into churches and schools everywhere and tell her famous stories. She'd even tell stories to the kids who lived in her apartment complex, through a ministry called the Good News Club. I didn't realize until my twenties that she was actually living in the projects. My grandparents were never loaded with cash, but they were rich in love and faith.

Along with becoming more accepting of sweatpants and being highly impressed by a homemade sprinkler system, growing older has also helped me look back on my grandma's life and ministry with a new appreciation. She spread the Gospel however she could until the day she died. She finished the race. I've come to realize how much the Holy Spirit worked through her stories then and even still works through them now. One of her stories has lasted with my sister and me longer than we knew it would when we were hearing it as kids. It's the old story of *The Tale of Three Trees*. No one really knows who wrote it originally as it was handed down through generations. My grandma's version will always be my favorite, though.

The story is about three trees growing on a mountain, and each has a dream for its life. The first wanted to become a treasure chest and hold the most valuable stones in all the world. The second tree wanted to become a strong sailing ship that carried kings and battled storms. The third tree just wanted to remain where it was planted, growing to become the tallest tree in the forest, so that when people looked up at her she would point them to God. After my grandma would tell us what each tree's dream was, she'd always say, "And the God who loves little trees said, 'Just you wait, little tree. Just you wait.'"

The years passed on and the trees grew, and one day three woodcutters came up the mountain and each chopped a tree down, much to the despair of the third tree who just wanted to keep growing. Unfortunately for the first tree, it was not turned into a treasure chest, but instead it was made into a feed box for animals. The same disappointment fell on the second tree as it wasn't turned into a mighty ship, and instead was crafted into a simple fishing boat. And the third tree wasn't turned into anything at all, just chopped up and placed into a lumber yard. "But the God who loves little trees said, 'Just you wait, little tree. Just you wait.'"

Then one day, the baby Jesus was laid into the manger, and the first tree realized it was holding the greatest treasure in all the world. Years later, the fishing boat was in the middle of a terrible storm, and Jesus, who was asleep below the deck, raised his hands over the waters and spoke peace. As the stormy seas calmed, the tree knew he was carrying the King of heaven and earth. The third tree was eventually used to make the cross Jesus died on. So every time people thought of her now, they would think of God.

I can't tell you how many times over the years this story has come to my mind. Sometimes when either my sister or I are in a moment of doubt or frustration, we will text each other, "Just you wait, little tree." The story is a reminder of God's faithfulness in our confusion and in our seemingly unfulfilled dreams. But furthermore, I've come to recognize that even the ministry of my grandma's storytelling is a symbol of the faithfulness of God. She was a faithful servant to God, and she would have been the first to tell you he was consistently faithful to her, but he has continued to be faithful even after her death. God's faithfulness to her continues to be revealed through her children and grandchildren. I was only able to see this after a lot of time had passed, but I can look back and see the prayers of my grandma still at work in my life now.

One Christmas, a few months before my grandma died, she told all of us grandchildren the tree story one last time. Someone in our family was smart enough to record it on video. I watched it recently, and in that recording of the story she said, "In each one of our lives, God has an important thing for us to do. And Grandma is praying for each of her grandkids now. She is praying some of you will be storytellers, too."

She didn't live long enough to see me ever start writing, but I am now a storyteller in my own way. This book is a testament to her perseverance and faithfulness. It is a testament to the God who loves little trees. Little trees who fail over and over, who give up on their dreams, and who can't seem to find the faith to keep growing. Little trees who lose the wonder as they stumble through stages of hope, cynicism, apathy, and restlessness.

There is no way we can comprehend or understand the plans God has for our lives, especially while it feels like we're being cut down and placed in a situation we'd rather not be in. But "God's gifts and his call are irrevocable,"[4] and the "plans of the Lord stand firm forever, the purposes of his heart through all generations."[5]

Even in all of our unfaithfulness and impatience, the God who loves little trees says, "Just you wait, little tree. Just you wait."

♦ ♦ ♦

Christianity can be a hard religion to be a part of if you like to surround yourself with a bunch of intellectuals. I'm not saying that all Christians are dumb. Some of us are. If you've read this far in my book, I think I've proven my point here. But I'm speaking specifically to the difficulty many people find in subscribing to a faith that deals with so many absolutes. Many modern, highly educated thinkers have a hard time embracing even the most common beliefs held by the average Christian.

As Christians, we believe in one God of the universe. We believe Jesus is the Way, the Truth, and the Life, and there is no way to the Father but through him—the Son of God. We believe he died for our sins and was raised to life again. We believe we will spend eternity with him. Those are core beliefs. Nothing new for any Christian. However, even those bedrock beliefs can be considered controversial for some 21ˢᵗ Century intellectuals. Who are we to say there is only one way to God? Who are we to say Jesus is Lord and there aren't other options? Who are we to say the Bible is the true, holy word of God?

While I was living in Washington D.C., the National Museum of American History had a display of Thomas Jefferson's famous Bible. Jefferson was a highly regarded intellectual of his era, and apparently, he was a pretty good rapper according to the *Hamilton* soundtrack. He was a fan of Jesus when it came to his teachings and philosophies, but he didn't view Jesus as the Son of God. Jefferson thought Jesus was just a nice guy and a good teacher. So he cut the Gospels up with a razor blade and got rid of all the parts about Jesus' miracles and claims of Divinity, but he left in the parts of the Gospels where Jesus taught on ethics and morality. What was left was simply a "code of morals."[6] He literally cut and pasted his own version of the Gospel. Imagine if he could see Microsoft Word today; his head would explode.

To some people, like me, this sounds ridiculous. He cut out the very core of Christ's message. Yet, I have to immediately recognize my own cut-and-paste methods with the Bible. How many times do I ignore something in the Bible because I don't want to think about it? How many times do I justify my actions by saying, "Well, at least I'm not as bad as *that* guy." I emphasize the parts I like, and I try to find ways around the parts that make me uncomfortable. It's easy to condemn the sins we don't struggle with, but if it's a sin that trips us up, we minimize its weight. We create our own Jefferson Bibles all the time.

My pride leads me to depend on my own logic and morals, and I waste my time cutting and pasting my life together. When my situation feels unfair or I'm feeling insecure about my status or accomplishments, I run in circles trying to find some semblance of purpose and meaning outside of Jesus. I'm repeatedly unfaithful to what I say I believe.

Before Jesus was crucified, he had to stand before Pontius Pilate, who was a Roman ruler in the province of Judea. Pilate and Jesus had a very interesting dialogue, especially given that Jesus was mostly silent during the entire process of his trial. Pilate was trying to figure out what Jesus could have done that was somehow worthy of death. Jesus said to him, "The reason I was born and came into the world is to testify to the truth. Everyone on the side of truth listens to me."[7] Pilate responded with what I think is an excellent question, "What is truth?" But standing before the very Truth himself, Pilate blew the opportunity and walked away before Jesus could give him an answer to his question. Perhaps Pilate didn't want to hear an answer because that would mean he'd have to bow his authority to the only One who was rightly worthy to rule. Pilate cut out the part he didn't want to hear and walked away.

In Chapter 8 we talked about Jesus praying in the Garden of Gethsemane the night before all of this happened. Let's go back there again.

"Abba, Father," he said, "Everything is possible for you. Take this cup from me. Yet not what I will, but what you will."

Mark 14:36

Having all the power in the universe at his command, Jesus submitted to the Father's will. "Not what I will, but what you will." Jesus had clothed himself in human mortality. Our human nature will always want something other than the will of God. It's a battle we fight every day. Jesus told the disciples that night, "Watch and pray so that you will not fall into temptation. The spirit is willing, but the flesh is weak."[8] The flesh is at war with the spirit. Our will is at war with God's will. Unfaithfulness comes easily for us.

So according to Jesus, we are on the side of truth when we follow him. However, the will of our flesh is in conflict with God's will, which is why we live in tension. Our spirit wants to follow God, but our flesh—our fear, cynicism, unrewarding desires—blocks us from letting our spirit win, and we run after our own goals and dreams. We chase down counterfeit comforts that can never satisfy us, and when we fail to get a hold of those comforts, we grow cynical and apathetic thinking God is unfaithful because we didn't get what we wanted.

Jesus sacrificed his will to God's will and became our holy sacrifice. So our wills and desires must grate against God's truth as we are refined and sanctified in our Christian journey. Like a river carving out a path through a mountain, we often feel the pain of the erosion of our wills. We must lay our dreams at the feet of the Dream Giver.

How do I know I'm on the side of truth? Because it hurts.

When our beliefs have no conflicts, that's a sign we are most likely believing some lies or doing some cutting and pasting. The Bible has verses I wish weren't in it because it would make this religion a whole lot easier to advocate to others. But I've proven myself unfaithful and stupid so many times so I'm going to trust the word of God over my inclinations, preferences, and self-righteous judgments.

"Not what I will, but what you will" is a simple prayer to say, yet so challenging to actually pray with sincerity. I pray it often, but I don't know if I really mean it. For me, I pray something more like, "Not what I will, because I know I'm dumb. But not what you will either, God. Can we find a nice spot right in the middle where I feel good about myself for asking your opinion but also still kind of get my way? What other options do you have?"

"Your will be done" is tough. It means completely letting go of control. How can we ever wholeheartedly pray a prayer like that?

We can't. At least not by ourselves in our own strength. We have to rely on the supernatural strength of the Holy Spirit. It's not our job to change our hearts; it's God's job. Thankfully, the God who loves little trees is patient with us.

◆◆◆

There's a well-known saying that gets associated with some of the greatest people of history: "They never met a challenge they didn't back down from." We often say it about people at funerals, award ceremonies, and all-you-can-eat buffets. We love a champion who never quits in the face of a challenge. Not surprisingly, no one has ever said this phrase about me, and the way things are going, I don't think anyone ever will.

I give up a lot. I frequently accept my defeat and move on with my life. When I was eight years old, I quit piano lessons after a month because my instructor ate Life Savers in front of me the whole time and never shared them with me. I also quit the Christian version of Boy Scouts (Royal Rangers) because I thought it'd be nice to one day actually have a girlfriend. I've quit some things before I even started them, like learning software coding. About two years ago, I set up an account for Codecademy because I thought it would be nice to have a skill like that on my résumé. Then I started looking at how much time and brainpower it would require of me, and now I just get emails from them every few weeks reminding me I still have an account with them.

Quitting can be quite liberating, and not every challenge is worth mastering. There are times we have to let go of our endeavors and stop fooling ourselves. There are times we need to give up. It's not always a bad thing to be a quitter. Quitting can save us from wasting valuable time, energy, and money. Remember that Austrian lady who died in *Indiana Jones and the Last Crusade* when she was reaching for the Holy Grail while the floor was falling apart? If she had only known how to quit, she'd still be here with us today. At her funeral, the eulogist said, "She never met a challenge she didn't back down from, but clearly she should have."

Tensions arise when we are faced with the decision to either quit or keep going. When are we chasing after the wind and when are we working toward something good that is worth pursuing? Sometimes I wonder if I've quit things I should have stayed with. Did I let go too soon? Did I turn around when I should have powered through? How do we ever know we're doing the right thing?

On the same night Jesus went into the garden to pray, he talked to his disciples about the Holy Spirit. He said the Holy Spirit would be their helper who would teach them everything.[9] He also said the Holy Spirit would guide them into truth.[10] The same goes for us today. We're not left helplessly guessing and feeling our way around in the dark. We have a Guide—the Spirit that points us to the Way, the Truth, and the Life.

We're "prone to wander"[11] and prone to make our own Jefferson Bibles. Yet in the midst of all of our pulling away from God, I've found he doesn't relent in his pursuit of us. He doesn't quit even when we quit. "If we are faithless, he remains faithful, for he cannot disown himself."[12] He's the Shepherd who leaves 99 sheep just to rescue one.[13] God doesn't give us a nudge down the hill to get rolling and then leave us to figure things out ourselves as we zig and zag uncontrollably on our bikes. The Holy Spirit is our guide, and he's actively involved in our stories as they are unfolding. Believe it or not, he cares about our passions and desires because he's the one who gave them to us.

Maybe you haven't quit Codecademy immediately after creating an account, but I'm sure you've felt like giving up at some point. Maybe it comes in waves during certain seasons of life, or maybe you feel it every single day on your commute to work. Like Joseph, we may end up in situations where we are wondering how we ended up where we are if God is supposedly for us and involved in our stories.

A little while back, I thought about quitting writing completely. Writing has always been a part of my life in one way or another over the years. In middle school, I learned to play guitar and started writing songs. I wrote youth group drama skits in high school, and I wrote various sketches for a local TV show in college. I wrote blogs for years, and now it's progressed into writing books. My writing has never turned into a profession for me, but it's always been a passion of mine, and I think God has called me to do it.

One evening, I started to ask myself why I had put so much time and energy into writing when it hasn't gotten me anywhere. I wondered why I had ever felt called by God to begin with at all, or if I even had been called. What was the point of all my effort over the years if I didn't have anything to show for it? I don't know what it was exactly, but it was probably the same types of lies I've fallen victim to so many times in my life, like the times when I was driving away from the prison in Gainesville or kneeling by the side of my bed at my sister's house. I was in the car with Brittany and working through these thoughts aloud. I announced, "I think I'm done. I think I'm just going to give up on any of these efforts of mine and thoughts about them ever evolving into anything of significance. I'll just focus on doing what I can for you, our family, and my local church. But I'm tired of dreaming." I went to bed that night thinking it was time to move on from it all.

I'd been working on this book at that time, and I usually do a bulk of writing in morning sessions. The next morning, however, I woke up and didn't really know what to do with myself because I wasn't going to be a writer anymore. So I rolled over and went back to sleep. A little while later, I finally got out of bed. I wasn't happy or mad; I was bummed. I thought I'd wake up with a sense of relief from not having to write because writing books feels like you perpetually have a homework assignment hanging over your head. But I had no relief, only a new uncomfortable feeling of uselessness. When I finally went to go sit down at my desk to start my job, I noticed a sticky note sitting there.

Please don't give up.
This means something.

- B

She hadn't left for work yet, so I went into the kitchen to thank her for her sweetness. Brittany said, "Your writing is more important than you realize. I mean you quit it for one morning and I can already tell you're depressed about it." I replied, "I know. I really am. I thought I would feel differently, but I feel even worse than I did last night." She said, "I think you need your writing maybe more than anyone else does."[14]

That made a lot of sense, and it was yet another moment where I was stopped in my tracks by God's truth. God has given me a passion to write, so who am I to say how my writing should be used? I had the wrong view of success. Being a successful writer doesn't mean that I need to have awards and a full-time career to show for it. If God's called me to do it, then just me sticking with it is a success in and of itself. So I am going to keep writing. It might change in the future, and that's okay, but I know it's what I need to be doing right now.

I'm such a quitter that I quit quitting.

God didn't give up on me even when I had given up. "If we are faithless, he remains faithful." We put too much pressure on ourselves to figure out our lives. We act like we need to know where we're going. We think all we've accomplished in our lives is a result of our superior planning or work ethic, but we can't take the credit for accomplishments when we're wandering quitters. The good things we somehow manage to pull off are only the result of a loving, active, faithful God. All we can do is give back our gifts and callings to the One who gave them to us.

We have no idea where our seemingly pointless efforts are leading us, and what they could already be doing. We're the unfinished, unfaithful wanderers, but "He who began a good work in [us] will carry it on to completion until the day of Christ Jesus."[15]

Perhaps the greatest accomplishments for the Kingdom of God show the least amount of success in the kingdom of this earth.

Just you wait, little tree. Just you wait.

Chapter 11

Regress to Progress

Starting from the Finish Line

"I care desperately about what I do. Do I know what product I'm selling? No. Do I know what I'm doing today? No. But I'm here, and I'm gonna give it my best shot."[1]

Hansel, *Zoolander*

Have you ever met someone who said they were a perfectionist, or are you a perfectionist yourself? It's an odd title to give yourself. It's always awkward when someone tells me they are a perfectionist, and then when I look at what they've produced I can't help but think, *Wow, we have very different definitions of what "perfection" means.* Perfection is an impossible goal, yet we often expect ourselves to be perfect. Perfection doesn't account for diversity. We're different people on different timelines, and we have different stories to live out. How do we even know what perfect is supposed to look like? Perfection is an elusive goal where we're chasing down an idea we've concocted in our heads of what it should look like.

In Chapter 5 I talked about my failure to be a perfect husband, but I don't think I'll ever be a perfect *anything*. We should probably never use the word "perfect" the majority of times we say it. Instead we should say, "Pretty good but there is always room for improvement because we'll never reach perfection." Go ahead and use that the next time your wife asks you how she looks. I'm pretty sure she'll respect you for your honesty.

We've come a long way in this book, and we've discussed a lot of the challenges we'll face and weaknesses we have to deal with in life. I want to be a better man, and I am actively working on myself and trying really hard. Even though I've identified my weaknesses and issues, it would still be absurd for me to expect myself to never again make mistakes in those same areas. I will be a bad Christian sometimes. I will be a bad husband. I will be a bad friend. I can chase perfection all I want, but I'll never attain it. I will fail over and over again. So I'm giving up on being perfect. I won't be able to pull off perfection. I'm not Jesus. I'm not Adele.

Perfection will always be out of reach for us. We won't be able to achieve all of our dreams, and many of them are dreams we shouldn't even be chasing.

So then what's the point of trying anything? Are we hopeless? If we can't be perfect, what can we be? I know we're supposed to strive to be better, but it feels like a race without a finish line.

I often grab lunch around town with my friend Mike Berry, and if you're keeping track, this is the third friend named Mike I've referenced in this book. One day we were eating at Chipotle and discussing our careers and not really knowing what our next steps would be. Did we really want to try to climb a corporate ladder to the top? Would it be worth it? How much time should we invest into our careers? How do we know if we've made it? Will it be enough when we get to that goal? And why do we keep subjecting our bodies to Chipotle's food?

We talked about the frustration of wanting to keep working hard, but not wanting our efforts to consume us. I said, "Where does it stop? Where is the finish line?" Mike thought for a second, and then he coined a term I really liked. He said, "Maybe the goal is to be *ambitiously content.* We work hard, but we work with an attitude of thankfulness instead of trying to get more for ourselves." I know, right? Pretty profound thoughts to have while holding a burrito.

This idea really resonated with me. I know ambitious contentment sounds counterintuitive at first, or like some made up fortune cookie advice.

You must run slowly to run fast.

You can't stop starting if you never start quitting.

You can get great songwriting advice from Fred Durst.

Ambitious contentment actually makes a lot of sense. Ambition is a wild animal. It's hard to tame and hard to keep under control. If you don't have any ambition, you're boring. If you have too much, you're obsessed with an idol. So working hard with an attitude of thankfulness is a realistic goal, whereas perfection is not a goal we can reach.

We can't be perfect, but we can still have peace.

◆ ◆ ◆

In Chapter 3 we talked about the story of Amaziah, the king of Judah. God gave him a miraculous victory in battle, and then he turned around and worshipped the foreign false gods of the people he'd just defeated. It's one of those stories where I wish I could travel back in time and punch some people in the face. Yet, as usual, I have to turn off my time machine and realize I'm more like the people in the story than I want to readily admit. And now I must punch myself in the face.

Amaziah blew his entire legacy and angered the only true God by bowing down and worshipping the very blessing God had just given him. But don't we do that all the time? Maybe not with wooden statues, but we bow down to our blessings constantly and in many different ways.

We pray for God to provide us with a new job, then he does, and we lose ourselves in it completely. We start to worry about it, and then we start to complain about it. Then we find out Karen from HR is at every new job we go to. So we start praying for a new job and the cycle repeats itself.

We pray for God to bring us someone to share a loving relationship with. Then he does, and we serve the person over God. Our time with God becomes minimized as we devote ourselves to the person who was at one point a blessing yet has now become a distraction, even an idol. Men often try and justify their idolization by saying their wives or girlfriends are "Proverbs 31 women." For the majority of my twenties, I had a "Proverbs 32 woman" in that she was nonexistent.

Unlike Hannah, the mother of the priest Samuel who gave her blessing back to the Lord, we act like Amaziah and serve the blessings. We put our hope in the gift instead of the gift Giver. And then, after time turns our blessings into our hindrances, we run back to God to fix it all again. We chase down fulfillment and purpose not realizing it is the same as chasing down perfection. It's an undefinable, unattainable goal, and all we end up finding are counterfeit comforts and quick fixes.

Jesus addressed this same issue in us a long time ago when he spoke to the very same people he'd just miraculously fed during the famous feeding of the five thousand with five loaves and two fish. Some people had followed him after he'd left the mass gathering.

Jesus answered, "Very truly I tell you, you are looking for me, not because you saw the signs I performed but because you ate the loaves and had your fill. Do not work for food that spoils, but for food that endures to eternal life, which the Son of Man will give you . . . I am the bread of life. Whoever comes to me will never go hungry, and whoever believes in me will never be thirsty."

John 6:26-27, 6:35

The people were chasing down bread for their stomachs instead of bread for their souls. When we chase bread that spoils, we'll never be fully satisfied. We will gain accomplishments and accolades, yet it will never be enough. At what point will we ever say we've had enough? When we chase down counterfeit comforts, or serve the blessings, we start hungering for food that spoils. Jesus is the only true *bread* that can truly fill us.

Why do we all do it? We do it because we've lost sight of the only One who can fulfill our heart's deepest longings, and the only One who can give us true purpose and peace. We measure our self-worth by our net-worth. We base our self-esteem off of what we think we can do for ourselves.

Amaziah never let go of his control, and so his gods never let go of him. Maybe the answer to all of these struggles is to merely let go. Let go of our wills and instead pray what Jesus prayed, "Not my will, but yours be done."[2]

◆ ◆ ◆

As I write this, I just got done eating too many chicken wings at dinner. My stomach hurts, and I feel gross. Lately, I've been trying to eat slower because I heard it takes a little while for your body to register that it is full from eating, so if you eat slower you realize you're full before you've eaten more than you need. Obviously, I'm not doing too well with that, and I just noticed we're out of Pepto-Bismol. My current situation makes me think about how King Solomon knew the pain of eating too many chicken wings, too.

> *I denied myself nothing my eyes desired;*
> *I refused my heart no pleasure.*
> *My heart took delight in all my labor,*
> *and this was the reward for all my toil.*
> *Yet when I surveyed all that my hands had done*
> *and what I had toiled to achieve,*
> *everything was meaningless, a chasing after the wind;*
> *nothing was gained under the sun.*

Ecclesiastes 2:10-11

Solomon amassed more than anyone could ever dream to have, in every sense imaginable. He had more wealth, women, and wisdom than possibly anyone else in all of history, yet he called it all meaningless. He was also the worst person to buy birthday gifts for. "Oh, neat. A candle. This too is meaningless." He chased counterfeit comforts and quick fixes, and all it did was give him a stomach ache.

Solomon was a victim of the same sin as Amaziah; he bowed to the gods of his accomplishments. Just like with Amaziah, I find myself falling into the same traps as Solomon, even though I have nowhere near the awards and honors Solomon had. Solomon had pride because of his prestige and wealth, meanwhile I take pride in getting my sprinklers to work.

Like an alcoholic at a bar, or me with chicken wings, or me in the discount section of Home Depot, or me at Dairy Queen, we never know when to cut ourselves off. How do we know when we've done enough or worked hard enough? When will enough ever be enough?

Solomon's writings in Ecclesiastes prove humans have been chasing the same winds and pursuing the same meaningless counterfeit comforts for ages. We're like lemmings jumping off the same cliff thinking we'll get different results. We think if only we could get to a certain level of accomplishments then we'd not have to feel lonely or empty anymore. Tons of successful people have reached their dreams only to tell us, "It's still not enough."

We can continue to chase down the wind, or we can realize purpose isn't something we can ever achieve because it's something we already have. We'll never do enough until we know we are already enough. And we can only know we're already enough if we know Who created us with a purpose before we ever took a breath.

◆ ◆ ◆

The Bible verse most used for pumping ourselves up is arguably Philippians 4:13. "I can do all things through Christ who strengthens me." Christians love it. We yell it before we run out onto a football field. We say it under our breath before interviews. We recite it multiple times before seeing family members at Thanksgiving. It's our catchy reminder that we can be anything we want to be, and we can overcome any obstacle in our way.

But if you look just a few verses earlier, you'll see that Paul wasn't psyching himself up before an appearance on *Greece's Got Talent.*

I have learned to be content whatever the circumstances. I know what it is to be in need, and I know what it is to have plenty. I have learned the secret of being content in any and every situation, whether well fed or hungry, whether living in plenty or in want.

Philippians 4:11-12

When Paul wrote "I can do all things through Christ," he was speaking about the power of contentment. The wisdom to look at Christ and then look at his life and say, "This is enough. I am enough." If we really want to quote Philippians 4:13 fully in its context, it would probably be more accurate to say, "I can be content through Christ who strengthens me." We will never find fulfillment in what we can do for ourselves, so we must humble ourselves before God. Humility isn't giving up our ambitions and passions, it's just surrendering them to God. Humility is saying, "You know best. Not my will, but yours be done."

When you know you are enough, you don't have to prove it any other way with your life. That's not to say we throw off all of our ambitions, but we can bet that no job title, no amount of friends, no status, and no dream will ever be able to make us content if we don't already have contentment through Christ who strengthens us.

So many people run toward a finish line they'll never reach as they pursue more accolades or perfection—a chasing after the wind. Contentment doesn't relieve us of hard work and ambition, but it provides us with rest. It's the peace in knowing the God of the universe loves us and has a specific timeline for us, and it's not our job to figure everything out or work hard enough to eventually have value. Contentment allows us to have a finish line we can reach.

"Come to me, all you who are weary and burdened, and I will give you rest. Take my yoke upon you and learn from me, for I am gentle and humble in heart, and you will find rest for your souls. For my yoke is easy and my burden is light."

Matthew 11:28-30

Jesus is inviting us into his true rest and peace. We are enough because Christ says we are enough. That's it. He doesn't love us any more or less by what we do. He loves us because we are his creation. The finish line is at the cross of Jesus. When he was crucified, he said, "It is finished,"[3] so that means there is nothing more we could possibly pay back to God. We are enough because Christ's death and resurrection were enough.

I am loved not because of what I do or don't do. It's a hard idea to wrap my mind around, even as I write it out, because I'm so used to thinking I have to earn love and respect. I have to prove my worth every day. I have to show others I'm important enough or fun to be around so they will like me. I'm so tired of trying to prove my value when Jesus doesn't require anything like that from me.

We start from the finish line.

Imagine you are making your way into the throne room of Jesus. You walk through the foyer of a great palace, and you're towing carts full of all your efforts and achievements behind you. You're there to present it all before him to see if he'll love you because of all you've done. But before you can walk into the throne room, you are required to leave everything at the door. The doorway isn't wide enough to allow anything else to fit through except you, just as you are. You have to leave it all behind before you can stand before Jesus. So you lay down everything you're carrying and squeeze yourself through the narrow opening. And as you begin to walk toward him, he runs to you. Before you can even say his name, he embraces you and tells you that you are his child and that he loves you. All your efforts and awards mean nothing in the presence of the King. There is nothing more to prove and nothing more to say. Everything you've strived for in life is nowhere to be seen. Every failure is gone. The love of the only One who is perfect drives out all fear, failure, and insecurity. He says you're enough, and when you look at him you actually believe you are, too.

We can only love Jesus because he first loved us.4We are not loved because of what we have done or who we are, we are loved because of whose we are. And we are his. We are loved because we are loved. We're enough because we're enough. We can stop chasing after the wind.

> *But whatever were gains to me I now consider loss for the sake of Christ. What is more, I consider everything a loss because of the surpassing worth of knowing Christ Jesus my Lord, for whose sake I have lost all things. I consider them garbage, that I may gain Christ and be found in him, not having a righteousness of my own that comes from the law, but that which is through faith in Christ—the righteousness that comes from God on the basis of faith.*

Ephesians 3:7-9

So what changes when we know and accept that we're already loved?

Absolutely everything.

When you know you don't have to earn love, you're free to love yourself and others. When you know you don't have to earn forgiveness, you are free to forgive yourself and others. When you know you don't have to prove your worth, you're free to live out your purpose. Though we should work hard at our jobs and work to improve many of our situations, we can know we're already across the finish line. We can live with peace because we know the pursuit of status and purpose outside of Jesus will only lead to emptiness and meaninglessness.

When we know we're loved without having to earn it, it frees us from pride and insecurity. We can't take pride in how good we were to earn love, and we can't feel insecure and unworthy of receiving love when it's already ours to have. It's a matter of grace and not a result of karma.

For it is by grace you have been saved, through faith—and this is not from yourselves, it is the gift of God—not by works, so that no one can boast.

Ephesians 2:8-9

We can be content through Christ who gives us strength. We can rest in his grace. It doesn't mean we quit dreaming and running the race. Paul also wrote in Philippians that he would "press on toward the goal to win the prize for which God has called me heavenward in Christ Jesus."[5] So we press on toward our goals and good works, but if we are in Christ, we have a different starting line. Our starting line is the finish line of the cross. We don't work for love, we work because we are loved. We can be ambitiously content.

Our dreams are not bad, and they may not even be misguided, but they do not hold the power to give us purpose. Those of us with ambitions can get down on ourselves if we're not massively successful in the ways we want to be. We may feel like a failure because we have to work a day job, and maybe we even think working a day job means we have completely given up on our dreams. But there are people who reach their dreams and then realize it's not all it was cracked up to be. Then, they end up burning out in the passion they used to love because that passion became their full-time job.

A few months after my previous book had been out, I went through a bit of a weird experience. It wasn't a smash success and every publisher and literary agent I'd reached out to had turned me down, so I had to self-publish it. It felt like when I was a kid and I had spent a long time crafting the perfect paper airplane, only to throw it and watch it immediately nosedive into the ground. It was thrilling to have reached my dream of writing a book, but it didn't burst open a new world of opportunity for me. It was out there, and it was a rush of excitement to see it, but the excitement faded pretty quickly. It was like I had just yelled out "JUMANJI!" and the entire build up to releasing the book and all my hopes and aspirations had been sucked back into the board game.

One afternoon during this time, Brittany was baking in the kitchen and I was playing video games in the living room. She looked over at me on the couch and asked, "If just one person was affected by your book or came to know God in a new and better way, would that be enough?" I paused for a minute, and she may have thought I was going to give an elegant, spiritual response. However, I replied, "I know the right answer is to say, 'Yes, of course,' but I can't help thinking if it were only *one* person then there was probably a much easier way to influence them than pouring so much of my time and energy into writing a book."

What?

Hey, that's her fault for expecting more from me.

It's normal to have a mix of emotions over our efforts and hopes and results that follow them. We don't have to lie to ourselves and say we don't care what happens or what people think, but we have to remember where our starting line is. After Brittany had asked me that question, I thought about it for a while and eventually reminded myself that I didn't write the book to be a successful author; I wrote it because I felt like I was supposed to write it. And then I watched the Susan Boyle clip a few more times.

However, after that moment I slowly began to tell myself, "This is enough." It started one Sunday as I watched my pastor, Derek, preaching to our church, and I thought to myself, "Man, he's really good at this. He could be a megachurch pastor. Though, if we were a megachurch, I probably wouldn't know him as a friend. Even though the church could grow, he must be right where he needs to be right now. This is where God wants him to be." I started to think about what Brittany had asked me, and then I asked myself, "What if this is my peak? What if all I do is work a corporate job in my little cubicle and write stuff only a few dozen people will ever read? What if I remain faithful to my wife and do my best to love and lead my children in the ways of the Lord? What if I stay involved in my local church and the small places God leads me to? Will that be enough for me?"

I had to believe it was enough. Because if I couldn't find purpose and peace with my current results of following God, then I was never going to find purpose and peace even in a wave of incredible success. Long story short, I'd basically just repeated the scene from *Rudy* where Rudy's janitor friend knocks some sense into him when he's about to quit the football team. Except I was both Rudy and the janitor.

> *In this life, you don't have to prove nothin' to nobody but yourself. And after what you've gone through, if you haven't done that by now, it ain't gonna never happen.*[6]

We get amped to say, "I can do all things through Christ! I'll go where you send me!" But what if God's dream for you is to be right where you are? Saying, "God, I'll go where you send me," is no more important than saying, "I'll stay where you have me."

Contentment doesn't mean settling. Accepting what God has called us to isn't giving up. We press on toward our goals, but we do it continually saying, "Not my will, but yours." We want to believe we can change any situation and reach any goal we set our minds to, but that's not true. As we talked about in Chapter 2, there are some goals we'll never reach. Sometimes we will never reach our desired destinations no matter how hard we work. But if we can't change the place we're in, maybe the place was meant to change us.

You'll never be enough in this life until you know you are already enough. You'll never have enough until you know there is nothing more you need than Jesus. C.S. Lewis said, "He who has God and everything else has no more than he who has God only."[7] If we feel like we're falling behind in the race of life, it's only because we have been running races from the wrong starting lines.

◆ ◆ ◆

Are you who you want to be? I hope not, because that would probably mean you're dead. If there are any dead people reading this, can you tell me how accurate *The Good Place* is? I have a feeling it's pretty far off.

Our lives are one continual series of missing the mark and saying "Oops, I did it again." It can be frustrating to know we will always come up short, which is why we have to keep our eyes on eternity. This ongoing earthly process we are under is leading us to indescribable, unending eternal results.

Therefore we do not lose heart. Though outwardly we are wasting away, yet inwardly we are being renewed day by day. For our light and momentary troubles are achieving for us an eternal glory that far outweighs them all. So we fix our eyes not on what is seen, but on what is unseen, since what is seen is temporary, but what is unseen is eternal.

2 Corinthians 4:16-18

I try to keep my eyes on eternity, but it's hard when the earth is as far as I can see. When I look at myself through earthly eyes, I don't see much worth saving. In fact, I don't think of Jesus dying for me specifically. I think of him dying for everyone, and I'm just one soul in the middle of the masses. I know I'm a sinner who doesn't deserve salvation, but God's grace is a little easier for me to accept if I see myself as one of the many receiving it. Just another schmoe lumped into the crowd. On my own, I'm not worth the price Jesus had to pay. But if he got a discount on buying in bulk, then yeah, maybe I was worth it.

But the overwhelming truth is that Jesus would have died for me if I was the only person on the planet.

If you asked Jesus, "If just one person was affected by what you did, would it be enough?" He would say, "Absolutely." Each one of us is not just one of the masses to him. We each have a unique timeline, a purpose, and a place in the Kingdom of God.

We are unfinished creations wandering around and trying the best we can to prove we're someone worth loving, and it's all a wasted effort because no one can ever do enough to be enough. God's unending grace moves outside of time and logic. We are loved because we are loved. We are enough because we are enough.

♦♦♦

There are many self-help books and blogs that can teach you how to improve your life. Whether it's about time management, parenting, relationships, or health, we are not short on information. Yet, just when you think you've finally mastered one troubled area of life, you log onto Facebook for five seconds and find out you've apparently been slowly killing yourself by eating Cheerios, or by not eating enough Cheerios, or whatever. It's always the opposite of whatever you've been doing.

There is a lot of wisdom out there, even godly wisdom, that provides valuable insight to some areas of life, but there is no advice that can make you a better person than the person you were already created to be.

When God created human life, he said it was good.[8] We were made in the image of God.[9] A perfect and holy God. A God who doesn't make mistakes, get in stupid fights, or completely lose it while working on a home project. All we've done since creation is pull away from our true nature. We think we're on a journey to become better people by working hard at it. We want to gain more knowledge, more status, and more self-control, but we don't need to progress toward something better if we were made good to begin with.

God created mankind upright, but they have gone in search of many schemes.

Ecclesiastes 7:29

We want to work hard to show our progress, but instead, we really ought to spiritually *regress*. We were made upright. We were made as good creations, but we've gone in search of many schemes, counterfeit comforts, and prideful accolades. We've walked away from who we really are and settled for who we have become. We need to go backward, not forward.

As much as I love watching children falling while ice skating, I think I love watching them hunt for Easter eggs even more. I have to fight off jealousy when I see them because I love hunting for Easter eggs, and I want to be out there with them. But some parents get mad when you shove their kid out of the way to get to the eggs behind the bushes. Or so I've heard. When my jealousy subsides, I love watching their faces light up when they find the hidden eggs in a variety of places. They are thrilled with themselves for being able to find the hidden treasures.

As we seek to become better versions of ourselves, and as we regress backward to who we were made to be, it's a lot like Easter egg hunting. We roam around life hunting for new tips and tricks to help handle our emotions. We stumble across therapy sessions and times of prayer where we can purge our brokenness and truly make some positive changes in our lives. We find hidden eggs of self-improvement and lift them up in excitement. "Hey, look what I found! I found a way to control my temper! I found confidence, security, and peace! I found who I was made to be!" But the truth is, we aren't finding anything new. We're only discovering what was placed there for us by our Father.

We can't discover what has been created for us. We can only uncover what was hidden this whole time. We're not going to find any new life advice or tips that will turn us into better people, we can only rediscover who we were already meant to be. And through the power of Jesus Christ, we can know who we truly are.

The End

Epilogue

Well, here we are at the end of the book. Or is it really just the beginning?

No, it's definitely the end. Don't worry.

I once heard someone say they start writing their books after they come up with a title, which was insane to me. For the two books I've written, I haven't been able to come up with a title until the very end of the entire process of writing and editing. I don't know what it is, but it's just really difficult for me; it's like ordering a pizza over the phone. (Did I already use that joke? Look, it's the end of the book, just act like I haven't said it before.)

I have a five-page document with book title ideas. The working title of this book was "Book 2," which sounds like the worst movie sequel ever. *Three years ago, his family was taken from him while he was reading. Now he's back to seek out revenge and grammatical errors. Coming this summer . . . "Book 2."* I got pretty close to calling it "That'll Do, Pig." I still think that one perfectly applies for my life, but I didn't want to get into a legal battle with Universal Pictures.

Ultimately, I settled on *Almost Already* because it sums up so much of the process of being a Christian. We're always improving and working hard to better ourselves, but just when we think we've almost made it, we fail. We treat life like we're climbing a ladder, but instead of simply falling down to the next rung, we seemingly plummet to the floor. Yet in the midst of our failure, we may realize we're not really at the bottom at all. Through the power of Christ, we can see that there isn't even a ladder. We're not earning our way to love and acceptance because we're already enough.

The love of Christ doesn't get us out of the hard work of this life, though. On the contrary, it inspires us to work harder. It calls us to be more and do more. However, we do it in an effort to be *like* Jesus, not to be *loved* by Jesus. We start from the finish line.

There is a verse that has been on my heart for a while now. So much so I had my friend Annie turn it into a piece of art I keep up on the wall in the room where I wrote the majority of this book.

Godliness with contentment is great gain.

1 Timothy 6:6

It reminds me of our true goal in life, and it reminds me that we can rest. We can look at who we are and what we have and say, "This is enough because Christ was and is enough. That'll do, pig. That'll do."

We're incomplete completions. We're failures and we're overcomers. We're the almost and the already.

The End (Again)

Acknowledgements

Brittany, my flame, my muse, my bae. Thank you for believing in this book, and thank you for the years of encouragement, motivation, and love. Thank you for allowing me to share some of our less-than-flattering stories of our real lives and marriage. Thank you for not being scared to hit the delete key in the editing of this book, and thank you for never being scared to help me edit the rest of my life. You're my teammate, and I hope I have given you even an ounce of the support you've given me. Thank you for staying married, even after this awkward book.

Steffan Clousing, thank you for all the editing you've done for this book, and possibly/probably all the work you did in the final production parts that happened after I wrote this. You're always a great encouragement and sounding board, and your wording edits are equal to the abilities of Geoffrey Chaucer. Too much? How about equal to Jeffrey Goldblum? Thank you for your friendship and all the theological, political, and societal conversations we've had and will have. I hope I can repay you in some way some day.

LeAna Kimball, I feel like this book didn't really start coming together until you got involved with the editing. You brought such a spark of creativity and momentum, and just dang good skillz! I am so happy you were willing to jump in, and I'm so thankful for all the hours you graciously invested into it. Your input was phenomenal and I don't think the book would have been the same without you working on it. So, I guess you have to bear much of the blame, too. Sorry. But I can't wait to help edit your books next!

Ben Lopez, you're the man. You came in clutch with the book cover design, and it's so insanely better than whatever I was probably about to create in Microsoft Paint. I was blown away that you were even pumped to do it. Thank you so much. Also, you're a way better graphic designer than Gabe.

Ocean City Church, thank you for the love and support and letting me be part of the community. I hope this book represents our church well. You know a lot about me now, so if you don't want to make eye contact for a while, I get it. Oh yeah, Derek told me that you can buy copies of the book for your family and friends instead of tithing.

Finally, thank you to _____[Your Name]_____ for leaving such a great review on Amazon and Good Reads! You are so freaking cool and way better than the jerks who didn't!

Notes for the Nerds

Opening

1. Schur, Michael, Katie Dippold, and Harris Wittels. "Time Capsule." *Parks and Recreation*. Deedle-Dee Productions, Fremulon, 3 Arts Entertainment, Universal Media Studios (UMS). 3 Feb. 2011. Television. Transcript.

Chapter 1 - We Started from the Bottom and We're Still There

1. *Father of the Bride*. Dir. Charles Shyer. By Frances Goodrich and Albert Hackett. Touchstone Pictures, 1991. Film.
2. Luke 6:45.
3. Romans 8:31.
4. Isaiah 64:6.
5. I know you're wondering what kind of dog Walter is. We get asked all the time because he's so cute. He was a rescue dog we found when I was playing a music gig no one cared about at a Jacksonville farmers market thing. We did a cheek swab thing where you mail in the DNA and we found out he is half Shetland Sheepdog, a quarter Shih Tzu, and a quarter some kind of terrier mix, which we think is Wheaten Terrier. I am now a weird dog person, which is someone I swore I'd never become.

Chapter 2 - Overlooked

1. Hurwitz, Mitchell, John Levenstein, and Abraham Higginbotham. "Top Banana." *Arrested Development*. 20th Century Fox. 9 Nov. 2003. Television. Transcript.
2. Horelick, Stephen, et al. "Reading Rainbow Theme Song." 1983.
3. Zechariah 4:10.

4. Fun fact: I looked up if you're supposed to capitalize "atheist" and there are debates about it on Reddit.

5. Acts 1:23.

6. Acts 1:26.

7. Durose, Matthew R., Alexia D. Cooper, and Howard N. Snyder, *Recidivism of Prisoners Released in 30 States in 2005: Patterns from 2005 to 2010* (pdf, 31 pages), Bureau of Justice Statistics Special Report, April 2014, NCJ 244205.

8. Matthew 25:36.

9. Matthew 25:40.

10. Galatians 6:2.

Chapter 3 - Great Mehxpectations

1. Shore, David, and Thomas L. Moran. "Out of the Shoot." House. 20th Century Fox, 2011. Television. Transcript.

2. By the way, here's the formula for a hit Black Eyed Peas song: (Partying references) + (Words like "Let's go!" and "Everybody!") + (More references to partying) + (Spelling out a few words)

3. Andrews, Julie. "My Favorite Things." *The Sound of Music.* By Writer Oscar Hammerstein and Richard Rodgers. Imagem Music, 1965. MP3.

4. *Jurassic Park.* Dir. Steven Spielberg. By Michael Crichton and David Koepp. Universal Pictures, 1993. Film. Transcript.

5. You *Jurassic Park* fans liked that word play, didn't you?

6. 2 Chronicles 25:9.

7. 2 Chronicles 25:15.

8. 1 Peter 5:5.

9. James 5:16.

Chapter 4 - Waiting

1. Fey, Tina, Robert Carlock, Dylan Morgan, and Josh Siegal. "Kimmy Gives Up!" *Unbreakable Kimmy Schmidt.* 3 Arts Entertainment, 2016. Television. Transcript.

2. 1 Samuel 1:8.

3. Matthew 27:46.

4.	Psalm 22:1.

5.	Lamentations 3:7-9.

6.	Psalm 27:14.

7.	Psalm 37:5.

8.	Psalm 130:7.

9.	Isaiah 55:9.

10.	Lewis, C. S., and Pauline Baynes. *The Silver Chair*. G. Bles, 1953.

11.	1 Samuel 1:10.

12.	1 Samuel 1:15.

13.	John 16:21.

14.	Peterson, Eugene H. *Run with the Horses: The Quest for Life at Its Best*. IVP Books, 1983.

15.	"Social Security." Social Security History, Social Security Administration, www.ssa.gov/oact/babynames/top5names.html.

Chapter 5 - Come Fail Away

1.	Lieberstein, Paul and Michael Shur. "The Job," *The Office*. Deedle-Dee Productions; NBC Universal Television, 17 May 2007. Television. Transcript.

2.	Galatians 6:9.

3.	Klett, Leah Marieann. "Joshua Harris Apologizes for Mistakes in 'I Kissed Dating Goodbye' in Powerful TEDx Talk (Video)." The Gospel Herald, The Gospel Herald, 8 Dec. 2017, www.gospelherald.com/articles/71699/20171208/joshua-harris-apologizes-mistakes-kissed-dating-goodbye-powerful-tedx-talk.htm.

4.	I asked Phil if he remembered this story and if they knew we were fighting. He said, "Oh yeah, we definitely knew something was going down! But don't worry, that's happened to us plenty of times, too."

5.	Matthew 14:22.

6.	Matthew 14:31.

7.	Matthew 8:10 and Matthew 15:28.

8.	2 Peter 3:9.

9.	Psalm 103:8.

189

Chapter 6 - The Thief of Joy

1. *This is Spinal Tap*. Dir. Rob Reiner. By Chris Guest, Michael McKean, Harry Shearer, and Rob Reiner. Spinal Tap Productions, 1984. Film.
2. Exodus 19:6.
3. 1 Samuel 8:5.
4. 1 Samuel 8:7-9.
5. One time I ended a call by saying, "Amen." Not exactly the D.C. way to manage incoming calls.
6. Luke 22:42.
7. Romans 8:29, Ephesians 1:4-5, Colossians 1:15-18, Jeremiah 1:5, and 2 Peter 3:8.
8. 2 Samuel 2:1.

Chapter 7 - Hey Jealousy

1. Fey, Tina and Rob Weiner. "Secrets and Lies," *30 Rock*. Broadway Video; Little Stranger; NBC Studios, 6 Dec 2007. Television. Transcript.
2. Answer: All of the Presidents were firstborns or the only child until President Trump, who is the fourth of five children.
3. Luke 22:54-62.
4. John 21:15-17.
5. John 21:15-25.
6. Matthew 23:11-12.
7. Romans 12:15-16.
8. Galatians 6:2.
9. Lewis, C. S. and Pauline Baynes. *The Horse and His Boy*. HarperCollins, 1994.
10. Like that one Carman music video for "Great God" where he is a knight in medieval times with the long, Michael Bolton-looking hair. Please tell me I'm not the only one who remembers that.

Chapter 8 - Mr. Blue Sky

1. Harris, Susan, Robert Bruce and Martin Weiss. "Great Expectations," *The Golden Girls*. Witt/Thomas/Harris Productions, Touchstone Television, 13 Jan 1990. Television. Transcript.

2. Electric Light Orchestra. "Mr. Blue Sky." *Out of the Blue*, Musicland Studios, Munich, 1977. MP3.

3. Michael W. Smith. "Friends." *Michael W. Smith* Project, Reunion, 1983. MP3.

4. Govender, Serusha. "Is Crying Good for You?" WebMD, WebMD, www.webmd.com/balance/features/is-crying-good-for-you#1.

5. Noyes, Betty. "Baby Mine." *Dumbo*. By Frank Churchill and Ned Washington. Walt Disney Studios, 1941. MP3.

6. Matthew 12:34.

7. U2. "I Still Haven't Found What I'm Looking For." *The Joshua Tree*, Island Records, 1987. MP3.

8. Romans 12:5.

9. Colossians 1:18.

10. Luke 5:16 and Matthew 14:13.

11. John 11:35.

12. Luke 4:1-13.

13. Matthew 26:47-56.

14. Matthew 26:38.

15. Luke 22:44.

16. Matthew 26:56.

17. Lewis, C. S. *The Weight of Glory and Other Addresses*. Macmillan, 1949.

18. Psalm 103:1-2.

Chapter 9 - The Hopes and Fears of All the Years

1. Zwick, Joel, director. *My Big Fat Greek Wedding*. Playtone; 2002.

2. Burton, Al, Gloria Loring, and Alan Thicke. "The Facts of Life." 1979.

   a. Fun fact: Alan Thicke was the dad from *Growing Pains* and Robin Thicke's dad. I didn't know he wrote TV theme songs. He was a talented guy, and a great father to Mike Seaver, a.k.a. Kirk Cameron.

3. 1 John 4:18.

4. 2 Corinthians 5:21.

5. Genesis 39:2, Genesis 39:21, and Genesis 39:23.

6. Redner, Lewis H., et al. *O Little Town of Bethlehem: Christmas Hymn.* 1923.

Chapter 10 - Faithfully Unfaithful

1. Charles, Larry, Bruce Kirschbaum, Peter Mehlman, Larry David, and Jerry Seinfeld. "The Old Man," *Seinfeld*. Shapiro/West Productions, Castle Rock Entertainment; 18 Feb 1993. Television. Transcript.

2. Peters, R. "Ageing and the Brain." *Advances in Pediatrics.*, U.S. National Library of Medicine, Feb. 2006, www.ncbi.nlm.nih.gov/pmc/articles/PMC2596698/.

3. Matthew 18:3.

4. Romans 11:29.

5. Psalm 33:11.

6. Tay, Endrina. "The Life and Morals of Jesus of Nazareth." *Monticello.org*, 1 Oct. 2014, www.monticello.org/site/research-and-collections/life-and-morals-jesus-nazareth.

7. John 18:37.

8. Mark 14:38.

9. John 14:26.

10. John 16:13.

11. Robinson, Robert. *Come Thou Fount of Every Blessing.* 1757.

12. 2 Timothy 2:13.

13. Luke 15:4-7.

14. A note from Brittany: "I just want to mention that this paragraph makes me seem like an angel, but the truth is that I'm the whole reason he was having those doubts and reached that conclusion the night before."

15. Philippians 1:6.

Chapter 11 - Regress to Progress

1. Still, Ben, director. *Zoolander*. Paramount Pictures, Village Roadshow Pictures, VH1 Television; 2001.
2. Luke 22:42.
3. John 19:30.
4. 1 John 4:19.
5. Philippians 3:14.
6. Rudy quote.
7. Lewis, C. S. *The Weight of Glory and Other Addresses*. Macmillan, 1949.
8. Genesis 1:31.
9. Genesis 1:27.

If you enjoyed this book, you might like my other one. It's available on Amazon.com in print, Kindle, or audiobook formats. It takes a close look at the divisive nature of our culture, what the church has gotten right and wrong, and where Jesus stands in the middle of it all.

UNBALANCED

SEARCHING FOR TRUTH
BETWEEN RELIGION & CULTURE
(and really good Mexican food)

JONATHAN TONY

22433454R00124

Made in the USA
Columbia, SC
27 July 2018